I am in reverence of Mr. Cayce's remarkable clairvoyant gift, which is akin to having a direct pipeline, so to speak, to universal intelligence about life and the complexities of the body, mind, emotions and soul. *Alive & Well* is dedicated to Mr. Cayce's spirit, and to the readers of this book, in the hope that each chapter will enrich their lives as it did mine.

Researching and authoring *Alive & Well* has been a nourishing personal journey of enlightenment about contemporary gifted healers who utilize Edgar Cayce's health care concepts in the treatment of their patients and clients. I thank the healers, metaphysicians, numerologist/astrologer and psychics who contributed their knowledge in lectures, workshops and interviews for the following chapters.

Some of my own health challenges and search for well-being are part of the theme of *Alive & Well*. I have written about my experiences so readers can gain insight into the numerous available alternative health care options that I have utilized which embrace Cayce's health care concepts.

I am especially grateful to Edgar Cayce for his legacy of readings which contain an extraordinary body of knowledge that is very much "alive and well".

•••••••••••••••••

Bette S. Margolis, educator, author and illustrator has worked as a freelance writer/artist for over 25 years. She is the winner of the *Guilded Quill Award* for *A Heart Full of Love*, a book for children of divorce. Her work has been published by national and international houses. She is editor and publisher of Bette's Books, Highlands Ranch, Colorado. Her articles on alternative health care have appeared in health and metaphysical magazines. She teaches writing and illustration of children's books at colleges and universities in the USA, and conducts seminars for children of divorce and their families on the art of creating peace within oneself, with family, stepfamily and extended family.

Alive & Well

Volume One

Into The New Millennium With Edgar Cayce's Health Care Wisdom

by Bette S. Margolis

Published by
Transpersonal ☼
Publishing
www.TranspersonalPublishing.com

Edgar Cayce Readings
Edgar Cayce Foundation

This title- Volume One: ISBN 1-929661-12-6
First Printing, April, 2003
Second Printing, Revised, January, 2005

Volume Two: ISBN 1-929661-13-4

For additional copies, retail, or wholesale quantities of this
book or other related books, tapes, and CDs, contact the publisher through the worldwide web:

www.TranspersonalPublishing.com

Transpersonal Publishing
A Division of AHU, LLC
PO Box 249
Goshen, VA 24439

Manufactured in the United States of America
10 9 8 7 6 5 4 3 2 1

....

FOREWORD
Bruce Baar, MS, ND (candidate)

I was nine years old when my mother told me about Edgar Cayce. She had read about Cayce's remarkable clairvoyant gifts in *There Is A River*, a classic biography about the great seer. Fascinated, I began a lifelong study of the largest most impressive records of psychic perception to emanate from a single individual. Transcripts of Cayce's 14,287 telepathic statements, given in sessions for more than 8000 people, are typewritten accounts, known as "readings". They were recorded by a stenographer in the presence of several witnesses, while Cayce spoke in an extended state of consciousness. The readings, given over a period of 43 years, touched on a broad range of subjects including: meditation, dreams, reincarnation, prophecy, suggestions for comprehending confusion in personal relationships, finances, historical events, guidance about the future and advice on illness and pain. Three-quarters of the readings were related to health problems of people seeking Cayce's remedies to cure them. Cayce would accurately diagnose and recommend effective, and often unusual health remedies, in minute detail, for someone he may never have heard of who was thousands of miles away at the time of the reading.

File numbers were assigned to each reading, report, and correspondence, and documented and cross-indexed under thousands of subject headings by the A.R.E. (Association for Research and Enlightenment), an international non-profit, non-sectarian membership organization headquartered in Virginia Beach, Virginia. The A.R.E. was founded in 1931 by Edgar Cayce for the purpose of making the readings available to students, writers, investigators, medical doctors and psychologists. Today, A.R.E. is dedicated to investigation and experimentation on information in the readings. They promote Cayce-related conferences, seminars and lectures, and facilitation of personal transformation through the study, application and dissemination of knowledge contained in Cayce's readings.

At the time of the readings, mainstream "expert" thinking contradicted Cayce's insights. But, like many other people, I found Cayce's insights to be scientifically sound. Contemporary scientists are winning Nobel Prizes for "discoveries" that Cayce spoke about more than 80 years ago. His amazing ability to help people heal the body, mind and emotions earned Cayce the respected title of "Father of Holistic Health" by the *Journal of the American Medical Association* (JAMA). Cayce was a consultant to Presidents Woodrow Wilson and Franklin D. Roosevelt. It was through the readings with President Woodrow Wilson that the League of Nations evolved as a way for countries to talk peacefully instead of fighting.

My youthful interest in Cayce's readings has continued for more than 34 years of my life, and will, I believe, be ever enduring. I continue to assess the readings applying Cayce's principles for good health physically, mentally, emotionally and spiritually to my every day existence. I contacted those that I could find who had readings from Edgar Cayce. Although many had grown old since their readings, or passed on, I spoke to their relatives, children and friends, amassing a huge amount of information on the interpretation of the readings and the unusual health products, appliances and remedies Cayce recommended for curing specific ailments.

For almost 20 years I worked for the largest medical company in the world, while simultaneously researching and personally experimenting with Cayce's health procedures. As Cayce said: *"Nothing happens by chance."* (Reading 5259-1(18). Because of my experience in mainstream medicine, combined with my knowledge and application of Cayce's health care wisdom, the A.R.E. invited me to become the exclusive world-wide supplier of Edgar Cayce Products. I accepted, and today we manufacture and produce these products to meet the requirements of Edgar Cayce's specifications.

The readings tell us that we have the ability to maintain excellent health by balancing our lives to include: a sound personal purpose for living, positive mental attitude, a good diet that is primarily alkaline, adequate drinking water, proper assimilation and elimination, meditation and prayer, moderate exercise and participation in recreational activities. To accomplish lifestyle activities and goals, Cayce recommended the use of certain apparatus'. One of these instruments is the Radiac (pronounced ray-dee-ack). Cayce first mentioned it in 1921, and continued to indicate its use in over 1000 readings for hundreds of conditions. Our company, Baar Products, Inc., manufactures the Radiac and other Cayce recommended appliances to match Cayce's exact guidelines. In reading 957-3, he explained that the Appliance was not magical, but when properly constructed corresponds to the law of physics which allows constructive forces to predominate and vitalize the system.

Reading 1800-4 describes the Radiac as a battery formed of carbon steel which becomes electrolyzed by ice, cold or water, and then partakes of the same vibrations which form the human body. The connection between the vibratory forces of man and this appliance produces an equilibrium in the human body, and this, in turn, enables the body to relieve any tension caused by a deficiency or over-supply in itself. It would follow that an excess in one part may be forced to assist the part deficient, by a unison of electronic forces, helping the body to increase its production and gain the perfect equilibrium. This action may be compared to sleep, during which the energies of the whole body are enabled for recuperation. Cayce said that the vibrations from the Radiac were good for "...*every human individual.*" (Reading 1800-15) The list of health improvements attributed to the proper use of the Radiac includes:

* Reduction of stress and quieting the body from within
* Normalizing body weight
* Improving sensory perception
* Normalizing blood pressure
* Increasing life span
* Normalization of kidney functions
* Vitalizing the system
* Normalizing heart pulse rate
* Balancing the body
* Improving meditation
* Normalizing oxygen content in blood
* Increasing blood coagulation capability
* Reducing blood impurities
* Normalizing rest
* Improving metabolism
* Normalizing iron content and electrolytes in blood
* Bringing us close to our life's purpose by
  connecting us with our Divine core.
* Merging the body, mind and soul with the holy trinity,
  God the Father, the Son, and the Spirit.

The Radiac is about six inches tall and resembles a pyramid configuration with two connectors at the top. Cayce's method for using the Radiac requires placement of the Appliance in a small container with ice cubes around it up to an indicated red line. Water is then added to the ice up to the red line which the Radiac sits in for thirty minutes. A wire and electrode is attached to the two connectors at the top of the Radiac and to the wrist pulse point; a second wire and electrode is attached to the opposite ankle pulse point. After the connections are made, it is important to lie down and be at ease while the Radiac begins balancing the electrical energies of the body. This process generally takes 30 to

60 minutes. Nothing distracting, like watching TV, is to be done during this time. Several reactions to the Radiac may occur, including relaxation or sleepiness. If either of these states are experienced, it is okay to fall asleep. But if mental alertness results instead of sleepiness, then meditation, affirmation, visualization or prayer are recommended. It is important to know that the Radiac takes on the vibrations of the person using it. Therefore, the unit cannot be used by more than one individual. We have heard from individuals, who have used someone else's unit, that the experience was irritating to them. But when they acquired a new unit, used only by them, they reported very positive results.

In 1987 the Fetzer Energy Medicine Research Institute, Kalamazoo, Michigan, conducted a double blind scientific study on the Radiac to determine the physical effects using the instrument. The study indicated that the Radiac had a measurable effect on the human neuroendocrine system. There was evidence of greater coordination of the circulation which relates to stress reduction, normalization of blood circulation and relaxation.

Another Cayce recommended instrument, known today as the Baar Wet Cell Battery, is a liquid battery which operates similarly to a storage battery. Cayce indicated the Wet Cell Battery for many conditions including Parkinson's, Multiple Sclerosis, Scleroderma, ALS, Motor Neuron Disease, Cerebral Palsy, Paralysis, Alzheimer's, Dementia, Down's Syndrome and Arthritis. Usually when Cayce suggested the Wet Cell Battery, it was in conjunction with massage, nutrition and mind-body application. There are many documented testimonials by people who have overcome various diseases and afflictions using the Radiac or the Wet Cell Battery. In David Atkinson's inspiring book *Hope Springs Eternal*, Atkinson writes about how he conquered Motor Neuron Disease, also known as Lou Gehrig's Disease and ALS, with the use of the Baar Wet Cell Battery. Mainstream medicine considers the disease to be incurable. Symptoms of ALS are: nerve degeneration leading to muscle control loss and often paralysis and an inability to swallow. The Wet Cell Battery is believed to regenerate nerve cells.

David Atkinson's book, and the books and articles about the positive experiences people had utilizing the appliances, created a growing demand for the products. I quit my regular job employment at a medical company to devote my time to building appliances, advising those who bought them on proper usage, and keeping progress reports on the condition of people utilizing these appliances.

A large part of my purpose in life is dedicated to bettering lives. If, by supplying Edgar Cayce's many health care products, according to Cayce's specific description, meets that purpose, then I will continue. The readings are clear about the importance of building the Radiac and Wet Cell Battery correctly so they will be useful - this is a task that Baar Products has accomplished. To accurately engage the Radiac and Wet Cell Battery, we are available to answer questions and assist in instructing the user on correct set up and application of these appliances to the body.

"*Alive & Well*" discloses the profound positive effect Cayce's health care concepts have had on people's lives in the past and continue to have in the present. The information in this illuminating book, will, indeed, broaden your horizons on Cayce health care concepts to improve body, mind, emotions and spirit. Ms. Margolis' enlightening book exemplifies how they are currently utilized by health care professionals and laymen throughout the world, changing lives for the better.

•••••••••••••••••

Author's Note:

For a complete catalog of Edgar Cayce Products contact:

Baar Products, Inc.
PO Box 60
Downingtown, PA 19335
1-800-269-2502
www.baar.com

•••••••••••••••

Please Note: **No portion of this Foreword is to be reprinted without the express written permission of Bruce Baar and Bette S. Margolis/Bette's Books, Highlands Ranch, Colorado.**

CONTENTS

1

ENERGY MEDICINE - HOMEOPATHY
Homeopathy or Hysterectomy?
Karl Robinson, MD, MD Homeopath

....

Homeopathic medicines are prepared from animal, herbal, and mineral substances. Unlike pharmacological drugs, homeopathic medicines have no side effects and are perfectly safe.

Karl Robinson, MD, Homeopath

_____

Dr. Karl Robinson is a graduate of Yale University and Hahnemann Medical College, Philadelphia, PA. He studied with leading homeopaths from Greece, Germany, Belgium, Holland, England, South America, Canada and India. Robinson is the former editor of the Journal of the American Institute of Homeopathy, and founder of the Texas Society of Homeopathy. He is a medical doctor and the only full-time classical homeopath in Houston, Texas.

_____

The readings state that emotions originate from the connection of mind and spirit. The way we experience emotions, however is through the physiology they create...

Eric Mein, MD
From: *KEYS TO HEALTH*

1

LETTER:

"I have been using the Edgar Cayce health readings for over twenty years but had never heard of using a small dose of olive oil to heal the colon. Upon reading your article, I immediately took a half-teaspoon of olive oil three to four times per day for just three days. I got dramatic improvement in my colon starting on the fourth and fifth day. I now plan to repeat this procedure in the future and use even smaller doses as my body does not seem to need very much at all. Many thanks for a great health idea."

WS via email

RESPONSE FROM DAVID McMILLIN:

"Glad you were helped. In fact, the principle of using small doses applies to many of the therapies recommended by Cayce. He explained it like this: *'Give the stimuli to secrete the necessary elements ... rather than creating for it the active forces in the body! Hence, more often it will be found that the activity from what is known as the homeopathic doses is the better; even of allopathic medicine!'* (276-5).

Homeopathic doses are often extremely small. Cayce was saying that small doses (or mild treatments) are often the optimal way to help the body heal itself. Minimal treatments tend to assist the body in healing rather than overwhelming the system. In view of this fact, it is curious to me that Cayce prescribed traditional homeopathic medicines so infrequently. However, he often did use homeopathic principles. Some of the vibrational medicines used with the Wet Cell Battery for regeneration are intended to stimulate glands to secrete needed chemicals rather than providing the chemicals directly. As the reading excerpt implies, the principle of minimal dosage can also be applied to allopathic medicines - a practice that modern clinicians could probably use more often."

David McMillin, MA, Researcher
Meridian Institute

HOMEOPATHY OR HYSTERECTOMY?
Karl Robinson, MD, Homeopath

I had always suffered from heavy, painful menstrual cycles that immobilized me. Pharmaceutical prescriptions and over-the-counter remedies suppressed some of my symptoms, but did not cure them. Between PMS, uncomfortable periods, and post menstrual low energy, I could honestly say that I never felt well. Doctors with the finest reputations assured me that eventually my periods would cease and my problems would be over. About six years ago, however, my uterine bleeding alarmingly increased to a nonstop flow. I visited a local ob-gyn recommended to me by a nurse. She described him as competent, thorough and knowledgeable. "You can trust him," she told me.

He put me through $1000 of uncomfortable tests. I had a $1000 insurance deductible. The tests revealed no malignancy. He advised that the best solution to stop the bleeding, as well as prevent cancer of the uterus, was a hysterectomy. He said it was a good idea to remove my ovaries, too, so I would not have to worry about getting ovarian cancer. I felt like saying to him, "Why don't you have your testicles removed so you won't have to worry about testicular cancer?" But instead I protested, "There must be a better solution." He insisted there wasn't.

"You'll have to face it," he told me, "there's no way to 'think' the bleeding away, and there's nothing you can swallow to make the bleeding stop." I felt trapped, frightened, and desperate.

Although I was aware of alternative medicine and health care, I had equated it with quackery, voodoo, or something that a California hippie from the 60s would opt for. Unfortunately, that thinking was a great mistake. It took a health crisis for me to turn to homeopathy, only to discover that it offered the safe effective answers I had been searching for.

I went to Dr. Karl Robinson for a second opinion after reading an article he wrote about homeopathy for a Houston health magazine. He explained that a well trained homeopath with 1000 or more hours of study at a reputable school is hard to find. Dr. Robinson has an impressive education and track record as a medical doctor and homeopath and has practiced homeopathy for more than 25 years.

As I entered his small office on Westheimer near the Galleria, I was anxious. I did not know what to expect from a visit to a homeopath and I was feeling ill, physically weary and emotionally tired of being a prisoner of my body.

Dr. Robinson's nurse greeted me. She had told me on the phone that he could help me, and advised me not to schedule myself for surgery. "I hope this works," I quipped, after she informed me that the first office visit was $225. "I'm running out of money." She explained that the first visit was a lengthy interview because it takes time, patience, and expertise to find the correct medicine. The $225 was better than the $1000 the ob-gyn charged me, I reasoned, especially if Dr. Robinson could stop the bleeding and make me feel well again.

I sat down, waited for my turn, and scanned the waiting room. He came out of his office. "Looking for me?" he asked, clinically observing me. "I don't know," I answered. "Who are you?" My attitude was less than pleasant. I've never been particularly charming during a bloody battle with my body. My attitude, I discovered, was important to Dr. Robinson. It indicated my mental and emotional state. He viewed it as a symptom or a clue in the choice of an appropriate medicine. "I'm Dr. Robinson," he said. "Are you an artist or a writer?" he inquired.

I was surprised. How could he know that I was a writer and illustrator of children's books? I wasn't dressed like a bohemian writer or artist. "I have been studying people for so long that I can often guess a patient's profession accurately," he said.

We went into his office. I sat on a chair in front of his glass desk. It had several homeopathic books on it that contained symptoms and their medicines. I told him about the hysterectomy that hovered over me like an ax about to chop me apart. I gave him copies of the tests the ob-gyn had given me. Robinson said he did not want to see them, but he wanted to know more about my symptoms.

"Tell me about the bleeding," he said. I told him the gory details. "Can you help me?" I asked. "I don't know," he replied directly. "But I do get good results with homeopathic medicine for uterine bleeding. It's worth a try before you submit to surgery." I agreed with him.

An hour-and-a-half of questioning began. There was no gynecological examination. Each time I answered a question he put a long paper marker into various pages of his books of symptoms and their homeopathic medicines.

He asked questions that doctors had never asked me before: How do you react to hot weather? To cold weather? Are you chilly or warm natured? Which side do you sleep on, right, left, front or back? How do you react to drafts? What are your perspiration patterns? Do you have sleep abnormalities? What are your dreams like? Do you have food cravings? What foods do you dislike? What are your hobbies and interests? Tell me about your work situation. What

4

do you want to do with the rest of your life? What is your present family and the family you grew up with like?

He was relaxed, pleasant and easy to speak to. I felt almost comfortable telling him personal things about the idiosyncrasies, addictions, compulsions and peculiarities in my family. "I hate to say this," I joked sardonically, "but I'm the most normal member of my family." He laughed, then encouraged me to tell him about my hopes, fears, worries and apprehensions.

"Are you afraid of death?" he wanted to know.

"I prefer life!" I answered snidely.

"What makes you angry or depressed?" he asked. "I don't know," I hesitated, not particularly eager to be totally transparent. He asked the question in another way, "Do you have any disappointments?"

"Plenty," I confided. "I've been divorced twice. And a long term relationship just ended; but breaking up is for the best."

What did my personal relationships have to do with my bleeding? "Everything about you is important to me in building a clear picture of who you are," he said. "What I know about you will help me select the correct medicine to strengthen your entire system, emotionally, physically and spiritually. The bleeding should then stop."

Homeopaths view disease as a disturbance in the mind-body complex. This causes an energetic disorder. Acupuncturists call this energy the "chi", a non-measurable, unquantifiable energy. It is this subtle energy that governs all body systems (i.e. immune system, nervous system, endocrine system, etc.) as well as its billions of chemical reactions. Correct the energy with the right homeopathic medicine and the mind-body disorder will diminish so physical, mental and spiritual healing can begin.

"Why is it I haven't heard much about homeopathy?" I asked suspiciously. "Is it something new?"

"It's about 200 years old," he smiled, "and today it is largely practiced in England and other European countries, South America and India." He told me that in the late 1790s Samuel Hahnemann, a young German physician and chemist, discovered the principles of homeopathy. It became popular in the United States throughout the nineteenth century into the present. "With the advent of antibiotics in the 1940s and 1950s it appeared that infectious diseases

5

would be conquered. But that has not turned out to be the case," Robinson said.

I still wasn't sure how homeopathy was going to work on me. He explained that he had to find a homeopathic medicine which was similar to not only the abnormal bleeding I was experiencing, but also to the other symptoms characteristic of me as a person. "Each homeopathic medicine has been tested on healthy people called "provers", producing specific symptoms in them," he said. "The same substance causing the symptoms can also be used to cure them when taken in a microdosage."

To find the correct homeopathic medicine was complex as there are about 2000 to choose from. At the end of the office visit, Robinson did not prescribe a medicine. "I need to think about all you have told me. Call me in the morning," he said. This was different from what I was used to, MDs writing a prescription and handing me a bill.

The following day he told me to come back to his office. He gave me an oral dose of liquid medicine, and a small glass vial of tiny white pellets that had been medicated. "Take two pellets twice a day for 10 days, handle them carefully and keep them out of the sun," he instructed. I was not to touch the pellets, but instead I was to tap them from the bottle into my mouth and allow them to dissolve.

An instruction book that Robinson gave me listed things that could possibly antidote the medication: coffee with or without caffeine, camphor, and eucalyptus were at the top of the list. The only thing on the list that bothered me was not being able to use fingernail polish if it had camphor in it. Luckily, a friend found a store that carried L'Oreal nail polish without camphor.

"Will something unusual happen to me while I'm taking the medicine?" I asked, still not completely trusting. He assured me that homeopathic medicines are completely safe, non-toxic, with no side effects. They are monitored by the Federal Drug Administration.

On the third day after taking the medicine my symptoms worsened slightly. The following day the bleeding tapered off. It continued to get lighter as each day passed. By the tenth day the bleeding ended and I was feeling fine. My spirits were high and so was my energy level. In fact, I even started training for the Houston Marathon, and completed 13 miles in the final race.

I still could not believe my good fortune. "Is it going to last? I asked Robinson when I returned to his office one month later. That was six years ago

6

and my symptoms have not recurred. I still have my uterus and ovaries, and the periods I have had have been normal, no pain, no heavy bleeding.

Still skeptical, I asked if the homeopathic medicine I took was actually a placebo effect. Robinson said it was not. "Homeopathy acts on infants, babies, unconscious patients and animals," he explained. "Also, many patients like you experience feeling worse before getting better even when they have not been told to expect it."

Since then my family, friends, and students have tried homeopathy under Dr. Robinson's care. My four year old granddaughter with reactive airway disease was weaned off her breathing machine using homeopathic medicines. She now has completely normal breathing. "Homeopathy does not always work for everyone every time," Robinson stated. "Like other doctors I have my share of failures." However, his patients were treated successfully for a variety of discomforts and illnesses including: allergies, sinuses, hot flashes, PMS, fibrocystic disease of the breast, mastitis, ovarian problems, vaginal discharges, painful intercourse, dysmenorrhea, turning a breech baby in the womb, sleep disorders, nail biting, and a wide variety of emotional disorders such as depression over the death of a loved one and grief over a broken love affair. Homeopathy can also help counter the effects of anesthesia and speed healing after surgery.

I have done a lot of reading about homeopathy. There is a homeopathic medicine for many illnesses. "Homeopathy is one way to get well but not the only way," Robinson said. "Conventional systems, herbs, acupuncture and other holistic health care work too."

One out of three Americans now uses unconventional medicine and holistic health care according to the New England Journal of Medicine, January, 1993. A study by researchers at the University of Pennsylvania revealed that the higher your level of education, the more likely you are to choose alternative medicine and holistic health care. Homeopathy was my choice. I know it to be curative for body, mind, emotions and spirit. It is safe, with no chemical side effects and was my answer to an unnecessary surgical procedure.

••••••••••••••••

*...there is within the grasp of man...an antidote for EVERY poison,
for every ill...if thee will but be applied nature, natural sources.*

EDGAR CAYCE
Reading 2396-2

••••••••••••••••

For Information About Homeopaths in Your Area Contact:

National Center for Homeopathy
801 North Fairfax Street
Suite 306
Alexandria, VA. 22314
(703) 548-7790

Contact Dr. Karl Robinson at:

4100 Westheimer, Houston, TX.
Suite 100
Houston, Texas, 77027
Phone: 713-621-3184

••••••••••••••••

Contact Dr. Robinson's School for Homeopathy at:

New Mexico School of Classical Homeopathy
202 Morningside SE
Albuquerque, NM 87108
Phone: 505-266-5265
Website: www.homeopathyyes.com.
Email: information@homeopathyyes.com

8

RECOMMENDED READING

HOMEOPATHY
Karl Robinson, MD, MD Homeopath
Angel Press, New Mexico, 1994

THE FAMILY GUIDE TO HOMEOPATHY
Andrew Lockie, MD, MD Homeopath
Simon & Schuster, New York, 1989

•••••••••••••••••

*...palliative (medicine) may be injected for a time, but half a truth
is worse than a whole lie, for it deceiveth even the soul!"*

EDGAR CAYCE
Reading 366-1

•••••••••••••••••

2

LAUGHTER IS GOOD MEDICINE
Dale L. Anderson, MD

••••••••••••••••

*We can...help others by bringing joy and humor into their lives.
The (Cayce) readings encourage setting the goal of bringing
laughter into the lives of at least three people a day.*

Eric Mein, MD
From: *KEYS TO HEALTH*

Dale L. Anderson, MD, FACS, DABHM (Diplomat American Board of
Holistic Medicine) has been a Minnesota family practice doctor, board-certified
general surgeon and emergency urgent care physician for over 40 years. As a
keynote seminar speaker, he prescribes Method Acting and orchestra conducting
techniques to over 125 audiences each year. Billed as "innertainment" at its
best, his one-man "medicine show" spreads a healthy "happydemic". Anderson
is the coordinator of the Minnesota A.C.T. NOW Project, a coalition of medical
professionals and dramatic artists who identify the actions and thoughts that
impact the chemistry of health. He is past president of the Minnesota Chapter of
the National Speakers Association and the Medical Speakers Association.
Anderson has authored: *ACT NOW! - Acting Techniques You Can Use Every
Day*; *Muscle Pain Relief in 90 Seconds - The FOLD and HOLD Method*, and;
The Orchestra Conductor's Secret to Health and Long Life. Anderson is the
creator of *Laugh Masks, Laugh Mask Postcards, Laugh Mask Greeting Cards*,
and the *J'ARMING Laugh Song* cassette, all of which are available on his
website: www.ActHappy.com.

LAUGHTER IS GOOD MEDICINE
Rx From Dale L. Anderson, MD

"Remember that a good laugh, an arousing even to...hilariousness, is good for the body, physically, mentally, and gives the opportunity for greater mental and spiritual awakening," (Reading 2647) said Edgar Cayce 80 years ago.

Throughout the years, the holistic benefits of laughter have been researched. For example, a 35 year scientific study on the effects of laugher on 268 Harvard University graduates, concluded that laughter is linked to overall wellness. One of the most celebrated accounts linking laughter and well-being is by Norman Cousins, MD, an adjunct professor at the School of Medicine, UCLA. The *New England Journal of Medicine* (Dec. 1976) published Cousins' report of success with alleviating a personal painful physical condition by laughing for 10 minutes a day. Cousins noted the power that laughter had to improve his immune system.

Positive predictable emotional and physical states have been traced to laughter. In 1938, the *Journal of General Psychology* reported that 100 laughs a day equated to 10 minutes of rowing or jogging. Other research has shown that a good laugh massages and exercises internal organs from the lungs to the intestines, and a chuckle or even a giggle causes the diaphragm to move up and down. Laughter also stimulates the liver to generate a greater volume of bile. It increases secretions from the whole chain of the body's glands. Hearty laughter draws air into the lungs, which is then vigorously released, aerating every part of the lungs, which is especially beneficial for respiratory conditions. During mealtimes, digestion and absorption of nutrients is enhanced by laughing. Clinical testing also suggests that laughter measurably galvanizes higher levels of PNI neuropepides. The group known as endorphins falls into this category. Endorphins are morphine-like chemical substances and are produced in the brain through physical activity, causing a feeling of euphoria. These inner uppers are "...2000 times more potent than morphine and they are legal," says Dale Anderson, MD. Anderson is a board certified general surgeon trained at the Mayo Clinic, and a Minnesota emergency urgent care physician treating the acutely ill for over 40 years. He says, "Endorphins, also known as 'runner's high'. They don't have harmful side effects, will not break the bank, are fabulously easy for the body to make and can be used all day."

Anderson presents laughter training workshops to employees of leading USA corporations, associations, and groups of "vintage people", his term for senior citizens. He teaches the art of how to arouse "head" chemistry with positive attitude, smiling, and laughter. "This course of action is a catalyst for the production of endorphins, and an entree to healthier living," maintains Anderson. Endorphins are responsible for: countering pain, diminishing inflamed tissue, relaxing muscle tension, abating fear, anger and depression. They also help reduce high blood pressure, and heighten confidence, creativity, optimism, and the ability to be sociable and physically active. Endorphins can improve appearance, decreasing appetite and strengthen the immune system by raising N-cells and T-cells. This is particularly valuable in the treatment of AIDS.

Many years ago, Anderson treated an actress for an assortment of aches and pains. After they discussed her symptoms, he found that her discomfort occurred most frequently when she was playing morose or testy roles. Anderson realized that in acting out her role, she "became" her thoughts causing transformation of her chemistry which resulted in her distress. His conclusions led him to do an investigation of related research about "acting out" the chemistry of good health. He read about Ivan Pavlov, a Russian physiologist awarded the Nobel Prize in 1904 for his findings on the digestive process in dogs. Pavlov discovered that ringing a bell while feeding his dogs caused their digestive chemistries to produce the same physiology or conditioned response as when he rang the bell and did not feed them.

A contemporary of Pavlov's, Constantine Stanislavski the Director of the Moscow Theater, created Method Acting by applying Pavlov's principles to actors, stage techniques, and audiences. Method Acting is still used today as a stage technique. It maintains that costume, gestures, posture, image, aroma, music, color, lighting and staging can influence the feelings of actor's and audiences.

Stanislavski was in agreement with the American psychologist William James. It was James who instituted the "Act As If" school of psychology: feeling follows action; emotion follows motion. "Skilled actors implement this concept with certain posture, facial expression, costume, grooming, breath, motion and thought associated with specific emotions," Anderson maintains.

The Minnesota A.C.T. NOW Project coordinated by Anderson, is an alliance of Minnesota health care professionals and theater artists. They identify theater techniques that play out on the stage of daily life to enable people to harness happiness. Their conviction is that "acting well" stimulates the physiology of good health. "Physicians now recognize that people who apply the "Act As If" concept by positive scripting, staging, costuming, and acting healthy and happy produce good health chemistry," says Anderson. Anderson also believes that a positive state of mind often enhances conventional medications. Acting like a happy person has also proven to be beneficial for salespeople who can encourage an increase in customer purchases by 17% with a pleasant smile and matching attitude. And waiters and waitresses who put on a "happy act" can make 27% more in tips."

Anderson traveled to India to study the clinics of Priyadarshini Laughter Club International. The club is a Mumbai-based organization started by Madan Kataria, MD, in March, 1995. Since then, it has grown in numbers and spread to other parts of the country. Although the majority of the club's members are age 40-plus, Laughter Clubs have become part of some school curriculums in India. Dr. Madan and his laughing team initiated a Laughter Club at St. Xavier's School by leading 300 school children "to...laugh to their heart's content for more than 30 minutes." Today, many school curriculums in India incorporate laughter for 10 minutes a day after morning prayers. "Group laughter is contagious and a tremendous tension reliever," Madan says. Morning laughter is recommended for children and adults "...to keep good spirits throughout the day by energizing the body with happiness." Laughter Therapy's other possible benefits for children include: less nervousness and stage fright, development of self-assurance, and greater sports agility due to increased vitality and enlarged breathing capacity. Another advantage to implementing Laughter Therapy is that it can affect an expanded oxygen supply, which improves mental functions, academic performance and positive life attitudes that heighten leadership ability.

According to Madan, children normally laugh at least 300 times daily which is reduced to 15 - 20 times a week in adulthood. Modern society usually frowns upon giddiness in certain circumstances. It is considered impolite to laugh or giggle in houses of worship, most formal work situations and at the dinner table. As a result of these social mores, laughter has generally been delegated to clowns, comedians and fools. But Anderson and Madan encourage adults to act child-like (not childish), when appropriate, and laugh and/or smile for the health of it, as often as possible.

Anderson's belief that "...the mantra of happiness is universal," was confirmed when he observed the chuckling Priyadarshini's Laughter Club members enjoying themselves despite their various maladies. Kataria and Anderson know that people cannot laugh everything off or always be happy. But they agree that the degree of unhappiness can be diminished by acting happy or choosing to participate in activities that create the chemistry of well-being. "I have not been able to completely cure a terminally ill person with laughter," Anderson says, "but happiness can always make a very ill patient feel somewhat better."

His Rx for laughter is: stand in front of a mirror and laugh for 15 seconds twice a day starting with an artificial "ha-ha" from the throat. Very soon, it should come up from the belly until you laugh hard, loud, raucous knee-buckling guffaws. But if it doesn't work, Anderson recommends faking it, because once you get into the part, the laughter will become real. The effects of a 15 second laugh last 2 to 3 hours from ignited endorphins. After perfecting your laughter routine, Anderson advises trying it with family, friends and co-workers. "Even if they begin by laughing at you, eventually they will be laughing with you," he explains.

There are also special instructions that he gives his audiences for smiling: when you are feeling angry or downhearted, force yourself to smile no matter how foolish it feels. Be mindful of the subtle changes in your level of relaxation, and watch for the unfolding of your awakened happiness. "Smiling is the least expensive, easiest way to fill an endorphin prescription from your inner pharmacy," says Anderson. "Even a forced fake smile will alter the chemistry of the brain, and pretty soon natural smiling will become habitual."

Many experts in the field of wellness are certain that people can only derive joy from optimum health if they bond in a meaningful way with friends, family, lovers, nature and community. It is a proven fact that doctors visits dramatically diminish by an average of 16%, and life spans are lengthened, when people connect with one another through friendship, affection for a pet or even caring for houseplants. "A simple handshake, comforting touch, hug, shared smile or laugh all have power to connect people in ways that are not a threat," explains Anderson.

"Laughter, smiling, and camaraderie aren't the only ways to fool your body into believing that it is happy," Anderson says. Many activities can invite the feeling of joy into one's life including: eating, exercising, cheering, singing and creative visualization. Creating an environment of colors, music and aromas reminiscent of happiness is another recommendation for encouraging the discernment of pleasure. Comedy clubs, funny movies, TV situation comedies, reading comic strips, and hanging around with funny friends are also highly endorsed for probable laughter or smiles.

And then there is *J'ARMing*, Anderson's coined jargon for arm waving to popular music. "Great symphony conductors do it - and they live five years longer then the general population," Anderson reveals. His book *The Orchestra Conductor's Secret to Health and Long Life* guides readers on the art of *J'ARMing*, jogging with the arms. *J'ARMing* causes increased blood circulation via arteries that simultaneously feed the arms and brain, and, in turn, expand intelligence. At his conferences, attendees are given a chop stick to use as a baton. Standing, they wave their 'baton' to the strains of inner and outer happy music. The contagious audience laughter accompanies the beat as the silent song of endorphins works its health improving magic.

Anderson leaves his listener's laughing with a quote from Dr. Seuss's last book: *Oh, The Places You'll Go*:

> *"You have brains in your head.*
> *You have feet in your shoes.*
> *You can steer yourself*
> *Any direction you choose.*
>
> *So be sure when you step.*
> *Step with care and great tact.*
> *And remember that Life's*
> *A Great Balancing ACT."*

···················

Laughter is the shortest distance between two people.

Victor Borge
Humorist - Danish Pianist

For information about starting a Laughter Club,
and Laughter Therapy training techniques
contact Dr. Madan Kataria at:

A-1, Denzil, 3rd cross rd, Lokhandwala Complex,
Andheri (w), Mumbai - 400 053, India
Phone: 91-22-6316426
Fax: 91-22-6324293
Email: laugh@bom3.vsni.net.in

....

Older people need not undergo a prescribed disengagement from life. Love,
friendship, a feeling of connectedness with others, and a sense of humor
[much laughter] remain critical to our sense of well-being. As time goes by,
we should not forget the redemptive power of smiling, laughing and hugging.

Alvin F. Pouissaint, MD

JOKES TO IGNITE ENDORPHINS

Psychics should be licensed. We could give them the regular DMV test, only
with silver dollars and pizza dough over the eyes. If you can parallel park like
that, you're a psychic: **Jerry Seinfeld**

The chief problem about death, incidentally, is the fear that there may be no
afterlife. A depressing thought, particularly for those who have bothered to
shave. **Woody Allen**

I tried yoga because I heard you get to do your exercise lying down, so I
signed right up for that. **Corey Kahane**

My son has taken up meditation. At least it's better than sitting doing
nothing. **Max Kauffman**

16

RECOMMENDED READING

THE ORCHESTRA CONDUCTOR'S SECRET
TO HEALTH AND LONG LIFE
Dale L. Anderson, MD
John Wiley & Sons, Inc., 1997

THE ART OF MIXING WORK AND PLAY
Steve Wilson, Ph.D.
Steve Wilson Company, 1992

COMPASSIONATE LAUGHTER:
Jest For Your Health
Patty Wooten, RN, Ph.N.
Key Publishing, Inc., 1992

GESUNDHEIT:
Bringing Good Health To You;
The Medical System and Society
Through Physician Service,
Complementary Therapies, Humor and Joy
Patch Adams, MD
Inner Traditions International, Ltd., 1998
(revised edition)

The purpose of the doctor is to entertain the
patient while the disease takes its course.
Voltaire

17

3

NUMEROLOGY AND ASTROLOGY
Chart For: Bette Shula Margolis
Prepared By: Sharon Hoery, Numerologist/Astrologer

••••••••••••••••••

Q - "What is my cosmic number?"

A - "Numbers, as indicated, are arrived at the better either by the numerology of the name, of the birth, or the general number for the sex and the date itself that may be arrived at by the astrological aspects of the date. As a general, or a combination of these, it is as has been given - see?"

EDGAR CAYCE
Reading 281-48

———————————

Sharon Hoery, well-known Numerologist, utilizes astrology for greater perception of numbers. As a child, she viewed numbers with distaste because she associated them with the quantities related to arithmetic, her least favorite subject. But as an adult, Hoery learned about the quality of numbers and their function in reading the road map of one's destiny and connection to Source. *"Omnia in numeris sita sunt,"* ("Everything lies in numbers") she says. "I am in awe." Hoery does individual charts and workshops on numerology and the basics of astrology. She lives and works in Highlands Ranch, Colorado.

When Gertrude, Cayce's wife, asked if the planets have
anything to do with the ruling of the destiny of men, Cayce replied:

*They do....In the beginning, as our own planet, Earth, was
set in motion, the placing of other planets began the ruling
of the destiny of all matter as created, just as the division
of waters was and is ruled by the moon in its path around the
Earth...The strongest power in the destiny of man is the sun...
then the closer planets...at the time of the birth of the individual
...But let it be understood here...no action of any planet or any
of the phases of the sun, moon, or any of the heavenly bodies
surpass the rule of man's individual will power.*

EDGAR CAYCE
Reading 3744-3(29)

••••••••••••••••

Numerology is the process of interpreting attributes intrinsic in a number. It was practiced by many ancient civilizations including: Hebrew, Greek, Arabic and Egyptian. Pythagoras, born around 582 BC, gained much of his spiritual and scientific understanding of numbers after traveling to Egypt, Persia, Judea and Italy to contemplate scientific doctrines and spiritual principles of cultures existing in these countries. Based on his knowledge, Pythagoras established the school of Mysteries dedicated to teaching four sciences: arithmetic, music, astronomy and geometry. Pythagoras believed that everything was number, in a practical and spiritual sense, and that all things in the universe were subject to predictable progressive cycles. He gauged measurement of the cycles with numbers 1 through 9, attributing meaning to each number which he deciphered through scientific observation and experimentation. His conclusions were: "Number is the law of the universe; evolution is the law of life; unity is the law of God, ... and patterns repeat themselves." (Multiply 111111111 X 111111111 = 12345678987654321.)

Every day numerology is utilized in advertising, architecture and in the wonders of nature. For example, the family name of Japan's largest car manufacturer "Toyada", is actually "Toyoda". But they changed the "d" to a "t" because in numerology the numbers attributed to the letters in "Toyota" add up to a number that is symbolically luckier than the aggregate equated to the word "Toyoda".

The laws of numerology manifest themselves in nature. They are attested to in the grace of a singular seed representing number 1, the equivalent of raw creative energy that can bloom into something beautiful or void.

A circle is the universal symbol exemplified in nature by the sun, earth, balls, planets and wheels. And there are the wondrous natural spirals that follow the 5 energy (seashells, pine cones, fingerprints, a ram's horn, our ears, fists, watery whirlpools and galaxies) and the Fibonacci sequence: $0 + 1 = 1$, $1 + 1 = 2$, $2 + 1 = 3$, $3 + 2 = 5$, $5 + 3 = 8$, $8 + 5 = 13$, $13 + 8 = 21$, $21 + 13 = 34$, and so forth.

Business corporate logos like TWA and Master Card utilize the double circle which is the *vesica piscis* or the birth portal representing number 2. The west facade of the Cathedral of Notre Dame, Paris, is designed as 2 circles, which are representations of one circle descending from heaven and the other circle rising from earth. Stars on many flags around the world are symbolic of the pentad or number 5, the regenerative number.

Modern numerologists interpret a person's God-given purpose and makeup through information inherent in the numbers of one's birth name, month, date and year. Veteran Numerologist Sharon Hoery also utilizes astrology for a more comprehensive understanding of a person's chart, as the following chapter demonstrates.

·················

CHART FOR: BETTE SHULA MARGOLIS
Prepared By: Sharon Hoery, Numerologist/Astrologer

"The laws and principles of numbers are the road map to life," Numerologist Sharon Hoery says. "And a person's numbers are in their *Life Path*, *Expression*, *Soul* and *Outer Mask*." She clarifies these basic numerology terms before she begins preparing my chart.

Life Path number is revealed in the sum total of one's date, month and year of birth. It is the number indicating what you have come to learn in this lifetime. "You will attract people, situations and events that enable you to learn and grow," she tells me.

20

Expression is characterized by the sum total of the numbers corresponding to the letters in one's full birth name. It indicates innate skills, strengths and weaknesses brought in from past lifetimes. "What if you are a new soul?" I ask. Hoery tells me that a new soul still brings skills, strengths and weaknesses to their first incarnation. A new or old soul has to journey up Jacob's Ladder, or the evolutionary soul process, and back. This is the path for connection with the soul self and the One. When a soul enters the world of matter, the laws of matter concerning every day physical affairs and temptations must be addressed.

The quality of *Soul* is expressed in the sum total of numbers corresponding to vowels in the birth name. "Soul is the eternal essence of one's Higher Self. It is developed by learning through experience for the purpose of being closer to God," she says. According to Cayce: *"...there are no shortcuts to knowledge, to wisdom, to understanding - these must be lived, must be experienced by each and every soul." (830-2)*

One's *Outer Mask* is derived from the sum total of the numbers corresponding to the consonants of the birth name. The *Outer Mask* is like wearing a coat of attitudes, either from past incarnations or from this lifetime. "We exhibit our *Outer Mask* as a survival tool, to endure in the world that one has chosen to come back into," explains Hoery. "The *Outer Mask* is what we let others see, and it can inhibit our inner growth."

"Each number, from 1 through 9, has a balanced or unbalanced energy vibration," Hoery says. "What happened to all the other numbers in creation?" I ask.

She tells me that in numerology you reduce down to the single digit. It is the final digit that plays a role in the story of who you are, can and/or will become. Edgar Cayce's reading 5751-1 explains that the sum of the values of the letters in a person's first, middle and last name gives a number that is significant for the individual. Hoery outlines fundamental vibrations of numbers 1 through 9 which have remarkably accurate predictable traits:

Number 1 -

BALANCED: Independence, Active, Creative Raw energy, Innovative, Thinking, Leaders.

UNBALANCED: Selfish, Aggressive, Stubborn, Domineering, Antagonistic.

Number 2 -

BALANCED: Diplomacy, Sensitive, Considerate, Cooperative. Positive Relationships.

UNBALANCED: Insecure, Over-Emotional, Shy, Fearful, Prone To Too Much Detail, A Martyr. Abusive Relationships.

Number 3 -

BALANCED: Enthusiastic, Communicators, Artistic, Self-Expressive, Open and Honest With Feelings.

UNBALANCED: Gossipy, Critical, Scatters Energy, Moody.

Number 4 -

BALANCED: Practical, Serious, Determined, Must Follow A Step-By-Step Process Which Is The Key To Success.

UNBALANCED: Rigid, Narrow Minded, Stern, Workaholic, Not Working With Step-By- Step Process.

Number 5 -

BALANCED: Charming, Seeks Freedom, Adventurous, Quickness In Thought, Disciplined, Stands For A Regenerative Intrinsic Vital Force, Commitment To Mankind.

UNBALANCED: Rolling Stone, Thoughtless, Addictions, Irresponsible, Destructive.

Number 6 -

BALANCED: Stands For The Cosmic Mother. Sits In The Heart Chakra. Gives Structure, Order, Form. Works With Perfection And Beauty. Nurturer, Teacher, Idealist. Believes In The Harmonious Beauty In Life.

UNBALANCED: Self-righteous, Slow In Decisions, Meddlesome, Seeks Perfection Like An Addiction, And Will Not Accept Anything Less Than Perfection.

Number 7 -

BALANCED: Spiritual, Analyzes Things. Thinker, Intuitive, Self-Perfection, Trusting In Self.

UNBALANCED: Cold, Silent, Repressed, Too Reserved, Lack Of Trust In Self.

Number 8 -

BALANCED: Executive Ability, Seeks power, Ambitious, Efficiency, '8' Is The Infinity Symbol Of The Spiritual World Balanced With The Material World.

UNBALANCED: Too Ambitious, Materialistic, Controlling, Vengeful, Passive/Aggressive Behavior.

Number 9 -

BALANCED: Philanthropic, Compassionate, Unselfish, Living High Standards And In All Things Follows Integrity. Teaches By Example, Follows Spiritual Laws.

UNBALANCED: Too Much Love Of Self, Demanding Approval, Failure To Use Talent, Prone To Addictions.

•••••••••••••••

Numbers are the highest degree of knowledge. It is knowledge itself.

Plato

Hoery tells me that a numerology chart comes to the final numbers that divulge one's multi-faceted individuality and purpose. When she does a full chart, she works with numbers and the astrology natal birth chart. This gives a comprehensive picture of the patterns influencing a person's life. A numerology chart is about potential and purpose in this incarnation. An astrology chart shows the planets, signs and houses that the numbers will be inclined toward. Numerology and astrology have dual aspects that can work in harmony or contention.

Each letter of the alphabet is associated with a number:

A = 1; B = 2; C = 3; D = 4; E = 5; F = 6; G = 7; H = 8; I = 9; J = 10 (or 1 + 0 = 1); K = 11 (or 1 + 1 = 2); L = 12 (or 1 + 2 = 3); M = 13 (or 1 + 3 = 4); N = 14 (or 1 + 4 = 5); O = 15 (or 1 + 5 = 6); P = 16 (or 1 + 6 = 7); Q = 17 (or 1 + 7 = 8); R=18 (or 1 + 8 = 9); S = 19 (or 1 + 9 = 10 = 1 + 0 = 1); T = 20 (or 2 + 0 = 2); U = 21 (or 2 + 1 = 3); V = 22 (or 2 + 2 = 4); W = 23 (or 2 + 3 = 5); X = 24 (or 2 + 4 = 6); Y = 25 (or 2 + 5 = 7); Z = 26 (or 2 + 6 = 8)

When Hoery prepares a chart, some of the energies that she looks for are: intensity (meaning many) of numbers, lack of numbers, the letter "Y" and the letter "W". Intensity of one number or of several numbers indicates a person's focus is very singular, like hearing only one note. This is characteristic of a lack of flexibility. The scarcity of certain numbers in one's chart indicates the need to learn the vibration of a missing number, which often is hard to achieve.

The letter "Y" is controversial in terms of whether it is considered a vowel or not, and also because the formation of "Y" is shaped like a crossroads. Hoery says she uses "Y" as a vowel when "Y" is pronounced as "E" or "I", if "Y" is internal, such as in the words lyric, myth, syllable, when "Y" is used as a diphthong as in the words lyre, type, psychic, or if "Y" is used as an "R"-colored vowel, like "ur" or "er" as in the words myrtle and martyr. She uses the letter "W" as a consonant when it has no phonic value, which is before "R", as in the words wrist, wrong, wrote, and when used internally as in the words answer, two and sword. "W" before a vowel adds an "oo" sound. This is a delicate vowel and changes the overall vibration in a chart. "W" is a spiritual letter pervaded with the qualities of responsibility and gentleness; in balance, W delivers wisdom. When working with a "W" in a name, Hoery first does the chart without the "W". She then reworks the chart using the "W" as a vowel which changes the soul number. "W" energy will become more active in a person's life as they mature and change consciousness," she says.

I give Hoery my full birth name and birth date:

Bette Shula Margolis - October 30, 1941.

She prepares my chart accordingly:

CHART FOR BETTE SHULA MARGOLIS

		VOWELS	CONSONANTS
B	2		2
E	5	5	
T	2		2
T	2		2
E	5	5	
S	1		1
H	8		8
U	3	3	
L	3		3
A	1	1	
M	4		4
A	1	1	
R	9		9
G	7		7
O	6	6	
L	3		3
I	9	9	
S	1		1
72/9		30/3	42/6

Birthdate: October 30, 1941 Scorpio - Water - Fixed

Reduce the numbers down to a single digit:

October   30   1941
                     10   30   1+9+4+1
                      1 + 3   15/6
                      1 + 3 + 6 = 10/1

•••••••••••••••••

Life Path   10/1

Expression   72/9

Soul   30/3

Outer Mask   42/6

•••••••••••••••••

················

EXPLANATION OF BETTE'S NUMBERS

Life Path - 10/1

Bette will bring into her life opportunities to utilize her creativity and uniqueness. Creativity means having the choice to produce art, music, writing, singing or self nurture and/or nurture others. Bette's ideas can be original and she can be a leader in whatever field she chooses. However, this does not come easily. She will "go it alone" at times because number 1's have to stand on their own and utilize courage, daring, will power and intelligence to reveal the shadow side of self, the side we are reluctant to show. There will be a tendency to be a martyr to personal family problems and situations. And at times, to combat the martyr role, Bette can become aggressive or over assertive, as indicated by the opposite pole of her Life Path number. She will have to exercise will power not to fall back into past life habits which lie in numbers 1, 7, 2 and 9, or her present Life Path could be impeded. These ineffectual habits, like giving too much of self to others, can undermine taking care of self. It is a spiritual journey in this lifetime for Bette, as indicated by the zero which is the cosmic egg containing all or nothing. Balancing the raw creative force of number 1 with the unlimited spiritual potential or zero is Bette's task. If attained, it will benefit her soul growth and the whole planet.

Expression - 72/9

Bette brings artistic talents to this lifetime. She is an idealist with a connection to the Divine. The loop at the top of the 9 is above the rest of the number. This indicates that she came into this world as a spiritual being who served others in previous lifetimes. Giving to others in this lifetime, is natural to Bette. But if her service is out of balance, then taking care of herself will be neglected. She is a diplomat and has a developed sense of integrity and intuitive wisdom. However, she is analytic and most likely has not learned to fully trust her inner voice in favor of believing that experts might know more then she does.

27

Soul - 30/3

As a child, Bette was not given the freedom to express her uniqueness. Her soul wants to speak and express itself in a creative way. By turning the key of creative expression, Bette will find joy and light in her life leading to the power of self finding soul-self. Number 3 is symbolic of the Divine child seeing and understanding a situation from both sides, and creating something new from it. 3's have a very sensitive emotional field dealing with self-doubt, fear of expression and the tendency to manipulate rather than stating feelings directly. These issues need resolution to prevent hampering the soul from its expression.

Outer Mask - 42/6

Bette presents herself to others as an orderly person who is in control of herself. She will be the diplomat in an effort to balance differences between others. And she tries to bring harmony and beauty into any project. Bette will work long after others have gone home in order to achieve perfection, even if it means not taking care of herself. 6 can be very set in its way, because a six has high ideals and knows how things should be. Number 6 carries responsibilities of the cosmic mother. She feels it is her job to take care of others, and has a fine sense of justice.

•••••••••••••••••

I tell Sharon she is amazingly accurate about knowing me through my numbers. "I have followed your Life Path destiny to interpret what is inherent in the symbols," says Sharon. "Studying number symbols can be done by anyone. But going into the deeper meaning behind these symbols is a journey of awe."

"How is it possible to find the energy from past lives in a numerology reading?" I ask. Sharon tells me the answer is in the expression of the full birth name. Each letter in the birth name has a number. Some numbers may be missing and some may be in excess. For example, if a person has an excess of number 1 in their full birth name, it could be indicative of bringing into this incarnation past lives of being self-centered, aggressive, forceful, a martyr or very creative. That raw energy inherent in number 1 is very close to Divine energy. If a number is lacking in the birth name, then its absence means you will need to learn the attributes of that missing number. An example would be, if 1 is lacking in vibration, then this person would most likely have a deficit of confidence in themselves. It could also indicate the potential to overcompensate for his/her lack of confidence by being aggressive.

"It seems like my life is a repetition of patterns with habitual rhythms of ebbs and tides," I remark.

"This is the experience of every person," Hoery informs me. "Our earthly purpose is to enlighten and enable our souls to move into eternal planes of higher consciousness."

She examines my natal-astrology chart (*See natal chart on the following page*) to interpret my numerology reading on a deeper level. It reveals how numerology and astrology are synchronized. "Your natal chart measures the exact position of the stars and planets at the precise moment you took your first breath," Hoery explains. She believes that nature will take whatever course is necessary, including cesarean section, premature birth or a birth that is theoretically overdue, for a person to be born in sync with the specific astrological calibration aligned with one's chosen life purpose.

According to my natal chart, I am not a stranger to spirituality. The North Node clearly indicates a connection to a past life in spiritual service. Hoery tells me that I have brought attributes from a past life into this one that relate to my capacity for helping others. "But in this incarnation, you need to let go of the mask as protector and care taker, and care for yourself first," she recommends.

Hoery explains that numerology and astrology are pathways which she has tried to explain simply so I can understand my purpose in this lifetime. "I have opened a peephole to you into the oneness of self and the Creator," she tells me. Her years of study, intuitive listening and numerous other strategic factors are processed when she reads symbols in the numbers and astrology of a client's chart. She tells me that it is the reader's responsibility to check and counter-check information received from a client during a reading. It is important to ascertain that the reader's attitudes and similar energies are not being projected onto the client. Hoery understands that looking into someone's chart is like opening the doorway to very sacred, sensitive and often buried habits and patterns. "At a very deep level, we all know the abilities and potential the Creator has granted us and what we are here for," she says. "But time and life often pull us away from our inner voice."

Hoery looks at my astrology natal chart and tells me that my rising sign is in Sagittarius, a fire sign. Fire needs to have movement and air to sustain its need for activity. However, Hoery advises that unless I own the fire energy, my desire

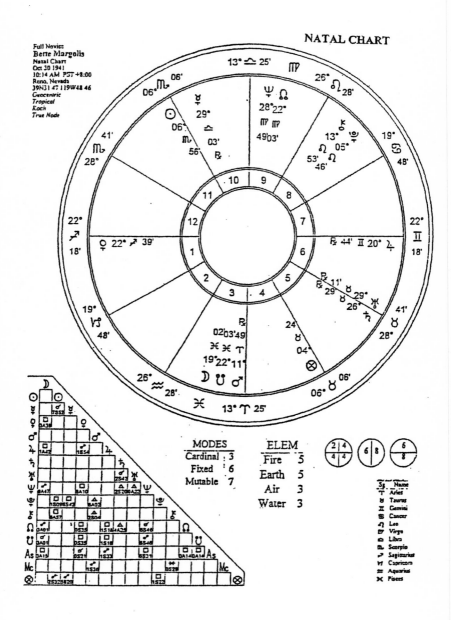

30

to see the vastness of the world will become synonymous with too many scattered interests. The result would be equivalent to never putting the puzzle pieces of life together. "To be successful you need to learn all details of one passion at a time," she explains. "This will open up other roads that you are meant to travel." I tell her that I have not yet learned to tame my desire to be involved in many explorations at once.

She continues comparing my numerology/astrology, pointing out that my natal chart is in agreement with my numbers. For example, my Midheaven in Libra (air) supports my need for balance which is reflected in my high ideals and keen sense of justice. Mercury is in Libra, focusing on a fine sense of thinking (represented in Mercury), which will keep things in harmony so they are balanced and beautiful. This is a very Libra characteristic. I tell Hoery that she is correct in her reading. I have always had a flair for interior decoration. My surroundings must be attractive or I cannot work at my optimum best.

My Sun is in Scorpio (water sign). According to Hoery, this indicates that I will search into the depths and darkness for answers to questions presented by the fire in Sagittarius. "Your natal chart tells me about a pull between the world view and the minutiae shifting of the scorpion eye," says Hoery. "You have such an astute ability for discerning what is underneath the surface." She explains that an inner tension will be ever present with these two energies and Libra's need to find balance and beauty. I acknowledge my intuitive abilities, an attribute that surfaced when I was a child. It is underscored by my Moon being in Pisces, a portent of being very in tune to what cannot be seen on the surface but is known intuitively.

"Your moon in Pisces (water sign) also makes clear that to find an unclouded projection of yourself will take disciplined grounding," Hoery points out. Pisces is very sensitive and can pick up messages on many levels as well as "junk" floating around verbally and tangibly. "If someone feels bad, you will tune into their sorrow and find that it clings to you," she tells me. I acknowledge that this is typical of me.

I learn that my Aries creates tension with my Sun which is the cause of often taking an impulsive course of action instead of properly planning. I also have Gemini, symbolic of communication, in the house of service under Jupiter's watch. This explains why I want to serve others by sharing information through communication. "With Taurus under the influence of Saturn and Uranus, you will receive tangible information that intuitively comes from another source," she tells me. "And you will spend time researching and thinking about this knowledge before communicating it to others."

31

Hoery concludes the reading by reaffirming that my astrology is in complete agreement with my numbers. It tells her that although I did not receive much support as a child in declaring my unique viewpoints, as an adult, I do. My opportunity in this lifetime is to honor my senses, the beautiful as well as that which repels me. This information is implicit in the Taurus earth energy. The challenge I am presented with is not to get stuck in the sensual moment and be controlled by it. "Take your learned lessons from the material detailed world to a grander view," she advises. "With Neptune in the 9th house, and the North Node in Virgo, your path is clearly defined as communication, in a big way, of the puzzles of the spiritual world."

I share Hoery's awe at the accurate wisdom inherent in numerology and astrology. Who else but the Creator could have engineered such a flawless life blueprint, with all its perfection and perfect flaws of who we are, and what we are meant to experience and contribute to life!

....

Know that in whatever state ye find thyself,
that - at the moment - is best for thee.

EDGAR CAYCE
Reading 369-16

All beings...down to the lowest atomic existence have their particular numbers, which distinguishes each from the other, and becomes the source of the attributes and qualities of their destiny.

HP Blavatsky
Renowned Clairvoyant

••••••••••••••••

Contact Sharon Hoery at:

Phone: 303-791-2512
Email: rshoery@aol.com

••••••••••••••••

Number is the Creator's foundation plan.

Jewish philosopher Philo of Alexandria,
who lived about the time of Jesus

••••••••••••••••

RECOMMENDED READING

THE LIFE YOU WERE BORN TO LIVE
Dan Millman
HJ Kramer, Inc., 1995

NUMEROLOGY:
The Complete Guide
Matthew Oliver Goodwin
Career Press, Inc., 1981

NUMEROLOGY AND THE DIVINE TRIANGLE
Faith Javane and Dusty Bunker
Schiffer Publishing, Limited, 1979

A BEGINNER'S GUIDE TO
CONSTRUCTING THE UNIVERSE
Michael S. Schneider
Harper Trade, 1994

NUMEROLOGY AND THE ENGLISH CABALAH
Shirley Blackwell Lawrence
Career Press, Inc., 1994

•••••••••••••••

Q - What is my soul number? Explain the significance of it?

A - Seven is the soul number. The significance is the
blessedness of the unity in activity.

EDGAR CAYCE
Reading 2084-10

4

HEALING SELF
Gladys Taylor McGarey, MD, MD (H)

••••••••••••••••

...healing the physical, without the change
in the mental and spiritual aspects, brings
little real help to individuals in the end.

EDGAR CAYCE
Reading 4021-1

••••••••••••••••

Patients are the sum of everything they think and
do, of their past and present, and their future hopes.
A patient is not just a disease or a disability.

Dr. Gladys Taylor McGarey, MD, MD (H)

••••••••••••••••

Gladys Taylor McGarey, MD, MD (H) is the child of medical missionaries. Born and reared in India, Dr. McGarey came to the United States at age sixteen. She completed her studies in 1946 at Women's Medical College, Philadelphia, PA. Dr. McGarey is well-known internationally for her pioneering work in holistic, integrative medicine. The famous "Baby Buggy Van", a vehicle she used to assist in home birthing, is her creation. Dr. McGarey authored *The Physician Within You,* and co-authored *The Stages of Stress Leading to Disease.*

She is the lead physician at the Scottsdale Holistic Medical Group, Scottsdale, Arizona where she is in partnership with her daughter Helene Wechsler, MD Recently, Dr. McGarey received the "Lifetime Achievement Award" from the American Board of Holistic Medicine, to acknowledge her 50-year contribution to the advancement of the healing arts. She is co-founder of the A.R.E. Clinic, Phoenix, Arizona, and past-president of the Arizona Board of Homeopathic Medicine.

...all visions and dreams are given for the benefit of the individual, if they would but interpret them correctly... "

EDGAR CAYCE
Reading 204-15

I am not a dream doctor. I will use drugs, diet or exercise
indicated for any health situation. But the best way we
have of convincing a patient of any therapy, however
odd it may seem, is to heal him/her with dream therapy.

Dr. Gladys Taylor McGarey, MD, MD (H)
From: *THE PHYSICIAN WITHIN YOU*

HEALING SELF
Gladys Taylor McGarey, MD, MD (H)

I am at Snow Mountain Ranch, Winter Park, Colorado with members of the Rocky Mountain Region of A.R.E. (Association of Research and Enlightenment, Edgar Cayce Foundation). We are waiting for the arrival of lecturer, author, visionary and holistic medicine pioneer, Dr. Gladys Taylor McGarey.

A woman seated next to me has traveled from Montana to hear Dr. McGarey speak. She has breast cancer but does not wish to resort to conventional treatment to save her life. She says she is interested in trying alternative therapies. Her hope is that Dr. McGarey will provide some insight on how she might regain her health. I talk to her about research and writing I have done on alternative therapies that have helped people effectively battle cancer. I suggest that while she is in Colorado, she attend a healing service conducted by Rev. Hanna Kroeger, the master herbalist. She asks for directions to Rev. Kroeger's "Chapel of Miracles" in Boulder, Colorado, and remarks, "It is fortuitous that we are seated next to each other." I remind her that Cayce said, *"Nothing happens by chance."* (5259-1(18)

Darlene Bodnar, President of the A.R.E. Rocky Mountain Region introduces Dr. McGarey by telling the audience that she first met Gladys McGarey at the A.R.E. Leaders Congress in Virginia Beach, Virginia. "I have been in awe of Gladys ever since. I love her personality, humor, intelligence, knowledge, healing abilities, the books she has written, and most of all, her cherished story telling."

Dr. McGarey walks to the podium. Her presence commands attention. She is tall, attractive, and stylish; her gray hair is neatly swept up with colored combs in a braided bun. She greets the audience and begins her lecture:

"I want to talk to you about the physician within you, which is the title of my new book. How do you make contact with the physician within? I had a patient who called me, and I misplaced the slip of paper with her message. It was Friday and I thought, well, if she really needs me, she will call me again over the weekend; but she did not. Monday morning when I got into the office, I found the message and I called her. She was mad at me for not returning her call, and told me she had consoled herself by thinking, 'If Dr. McGarey had called me back, I think she would have said that I had a vaginal infection.' But when she went to another doctor, he diagnosed her with a bladder infection. She told him she thought it was a vaginal infection. He rechecked her and found her diagnosis was correct. What happened was that when she could not get in touch with the physician outside her, she got in touch with the physician within her who had the answer. Then she was able to tell her doctor what the problem was.

"Nothing is more exciting to me than working with a patient who discovers that they are in charge of what is going on within their being. There is a lovely quote from Dr. Elisabeth Kubler-Ross, 'People are like stained glass windows, they sparkle and shine when the sun is out. But when darkness sets in, their true beauty is revealed, only if there is a light from within.' It is this light from within that we are looking for when we talk about contacting the physician inside us.

"How do we contact that magnificent being, the physician within us? First, we need to acknowledge the existence of the physician inside us. Then we can go about the business of contacting that physician within. A great way to do this is through body message or bodywork in general. Body contact is an aid in releasing memory patterns, and awakening the physician within. The body needs, wants, and asks for attention.

"I remember a 68-year old patient of mine, a pioneer nurse, who had answered everyone's problems but her own. She was suffering from abdominal and muscle pain. I sent her across the hall for a massage. The massage therapist ran over to tell me that he must have done something terribly wrong, the patient was sobbing uncontrollably. We handed her a box of tissues, and she told us that five people in her family had died in the prior year. But she had not allowed herself to grieve because she felt it would be a sign of weakness. The massage released her emotions, allowing her to get in touch with the physician within so the healing process could begin.

"Patients are not just their disease. They are the result of their thoughts, past, present, and future, and the sum of their experiences in life. I work with the whole patient, physical, mental, emotional and spiritual. Edgar Cayce said, *'Spirit is the life, mind is the builder, and the physical is the result.'* (349-4 (11). This concept is the foundation of my medical practice.

"I learned that mind is the builder when I was a 12-year old kid in India. I remember waking up one morning and thinking to myself, 'There's something wrong, I don't have any friends.' I am a Sagittarius, and when kids made me mad, I punched them out. I knew that I had better do something about my attitude, or I was going to have a miserable life ahead of me. I thought about the difference between me and my mother; everyone loved my mother. She had the ability to put gentle humor into any predicament making unpleasant experiences acceptable. I decided to be more like her and find a bright spot in every situation. I told myself that I was not a mean, nasty, hateful kid, and it worked; I began making friends. We can turn our lives around at any stage of our existence. Everyday we have a choice in our outlook on life, and how we deal with circumstances. Our decisions effect who we are, physically, mentally, emotionally and spiritually.

"What we think, we become. When life pushes me into a tight spot, I think of one of hundreds of Edgar Cayce's affirmations expressing an ideal. I have memorized many of them, and they have been like lifelines for me. For example, *'Not my will but Thine, O Lord, be done in me and through me. Let me ever be a channel of blessings, today, now, to those that I contact in every way. Let my going in and my coming out, be in accord with that Thou would have me do, and as the call comes, 'Here am I, send me, use me.'* (262-3). Or, *'Father, as we seek to see and know Thy face, may we each, as individuals and as a group, come to know ourselves, even as we are known, that we as lights in Thee may give the better concept of Thy Spirit in this world.'* (262-5)

"Another way of getting in touch with the physician within is through dreams. I had a patient who had a lesion on her chest for years and had seen many doctors about it. I did not think it was a bad problem because it was not oozing or itching; and she could have worn a blouse to cover it up. But it was a problem for her. I suggested placing castor oil packs on the lesion to shrink it, but she didn't do that. So I asked her to pay attention to her dreams.

"Dreams are a great resource for understanding ourselves. They inform us about things that effect our health. Edgar Cayce said, *'Dreams are a manifestation of the subconscious. Any personal condition before becoming a reality is first dreamed.'* (136-18). I will do whatever a health situation demands: dreams, conventional drugs or alternative therapies. But I have found that one of the best ways to begin a patient's healing is to access the physician within through the patient's dreams.

"She came back a month later and told me that she had dreamt black and white dreams: a nun in a black habit, a bride in a white dress, a black cat, a white cat. I asked her if she grew up in a rigid black and white world. Her answer was yes, she was raised as a strict Catholic with no gray areas. Life in her home was viewed as absolutely right or absolutely wrong.

"I asked her to tell me how the lesion started. The story was that when she was 17 she had attended a graduation party on the beach and gotten severely sunburned. It cleared up, except for one spot where the lesion appeared. During that summer she had gotten into drinking, drugs, and had an abortion. Her emotional problems lasted for years. Then she got married and her life seemed fine, except for the lesion on her chest. I examined it again; the lesion looked like a perfect upside-down letter "A". I asked her if she had read *The Scarlet Letter* by Hawthorne before she graduated from high school. She said that she had. It took me awhile to realize why the "A" was upside-down. It was because nobody was calling her an adulteress except herself. That is what she had affirmed and that was what her body was giving her. The body is only a representation of what our mind tells us to do with it. And so, we began working on forgiveness and acceptance.

"Illness is another method of getting in touch with the physician within. It is an acceptable way of allowing ourselves and the world around us to know that there is something wrong and that something needs to be done about it. Comedian Woody Allen said, 'I don't get depressed, I grow a tumor!' Illness gets our attention just like pain does.

"There are more pain medicines advertised on television than any other type of ad. The headache industry alone is a seventy-two billion dollar a year industry. Pain is a messenger that lets us know what is going on inside us. If we are hurting, we are alive and connected. If we do not feel pain, we are dead or anesthetized in some way.

"The other day, my 7-year old grandson came into my house screaming. He had smashed his fingers in the car door. My daughter Helene and I tried to get him to let us see his fingers. But he looked at us and shouted, 'No! No! They are my fingers and I am in charge of them.' Now that kid is really connected!

"And then there is mental and emotional pain. I remember a mother who came to my office because she needed someone to talk to her 15-year old daughter who was driving her nuts. One day she and her daughter were going at it. In the middle of this tirade, her daughter looked at her and said, 'I'm so glad you are my mother. I don't know anyone else who would be willing to hang on to me right now.' And then she went right back into ranting. You see, it was essential for that kid to know that she was emotionally connected.

"There is nothing worse than spiritual pain because when you are cut off from your source of connection, you enter the dark night of the soul. You may have read about my patient, Dr. Elisabeth Kubler-Ross, and her two year struggle with the dark night of her soul. She has been mad at God, angry at Him before the whole world. But since April, she has worked with a healer and things have begun to turn around for her. Elisabeth told me that on her birthday, June 8th, Jesus said that it was time for her to stop fussing with death and begin working with life again. So she has reconnected with God.

"Edgar Cayce said, *'In suffering STRENGTH is gained.'* (5528-1) Elisabeth's period of suffering has given her a dimension of understanding which now enables her to help others going through a dark period in their lives. The beautiful thing about this is that people all over the world are writing to Elisabeth to say that her experience has given them courage to live through their soul suffering. And it is absolutely awesome to watch people emerge from emotional darkness, and connect with the spiritual aspect of themselves. That is when the healing process begins.

"Do you know that there isn't any physician who does healing? I have watched beautiful jobs of surgery that don't heal and botched up jobs that heal very well. So who does the healing? It is not the physician, but the patient. Edgar Cayce said, *'For who healeth all thy diseases? If ye think it is the doctor or the surgeon, who is thy doctor? Is his life different from your own?'* (3684-1)

"A 72-year-old patient of mine had osteosarcoma of the shoulder which had to be removed. Then the cancer spread to his lungs. He dreamt that he was pinned to the earth with four large wooden pegs, symbols of the powers of the earth. They told him that he could not get up. 'You are wrong!' he insisted. 'I have 12 powers of the mind and I will get up.' That summer he bought 12 white turkeys, and he fed them grasshoppers. He told the turkeys that they were his white blood cells and the grasshoppers were his cancer cells. When Thanksgiving came, he sold his turkeys. At Christmas he developed pneumonia, and in January he died. On autopsy they found no cancer. It is amazing what we can do when we get in touch with the spiritual part of ourselves.

41

"In order to work with the physician within, we need positive support systems. I don't know how I would get along without my Search For God Study Group. I have had a study group in my home since 1956. The depth of communication that we get into, and the ongoing connection, is vital to me. Sometimes all we do is tell each other what a lousy day it was. We need support groups of people who will help us get through our predicaments.

"I remember a patient of mine who was constitutionally inadequate; she was always sick. When she was 40 she became pregnant for the first time. With a great deal of soul searching she decided to go through with the pregnancy. At about two-and-a-half months her amniocentesis test showed she had a severely defective child. After praying for the right decision, she decided to have an abortion. When it was over, a woman from her prayer group phoned her and shouted, 'Murderer!' That kind of support we do not need. We need people who will help us through our pain.

"On my 70th birthday, my grandson asked me how old I was. 'Well, Daniel, I am 70,' I told him.

'Is that old, Nanni?' he wanted to know.

'Some people think it is,' I said.

'I'm 4. And when you get to be really old and really sick, I am going to come up to your room, and pick you up and rock you in my arms.'

"Now, I know that he has a little book that tells that story. But the important thing is that he said it to me at a time when I needed to have it said. And I know that he will never remember it, but I will never forget it. It is vital to me to have that kind of support.

"Still another way of working with the physician within is balance. The Cayce readings talk about balance over and over again: balance between the sympathetic and parasympathetic nervous system, balance between the liver and the spleen, balance of assimilations and eliminations. To stay well on all levels of our being, spiritual, emotional, mental and physical, balance is essential. If all you do is take in and don't give out, it is deadly. If you receive love but you don't give love, the relationship will go nowhere. And if all you do is eat, but you don't eliminate, you are going to die. Yet there isn't anyone who is totally well. Everyone I know has corns or constipation. Jesus had it made! The rest of us all have something. But we should not feel guilty about it. We just need to find solutions for balancing the body, emotions, mind and spirit.

"My friend Alice suffers from chronic arthritic pain. She had a dream in which she saw a three sided square. Men don't understand a three sided square, but women do! In one corner of the three sided square there was beauty; in another there was pain; and in another corner there was love, stress and confusion. She was zapping these corners together in her dream, connecting pain with beauty, and stress and confusion with love. Her dream said that pain can be balanced by being involved with beauty, and stress and confusion can be balanced with love. The following week, Alice and I went to the symphony. She was having a lot of discomfort, but as she listened to the compositions by Strauss, her pain dissipated and she was comfortable for more than five hours. Alice went beyond herself by concentrating on the beauty of the music, an experience that lifted her out of pain for many hours.

"Accepting death is yet another way of working with the physician within. We are all going to die. Death is part of the overall scheme of things. Physicians often feel that they have failed when a patient dies. Whom do we doctors think we are? We can't keep everyone alive.

"My Dad was a great guy, a staunch Scotch Presbyterian, very zealous. When my mother died, he married my brother's mother-in-law. That made my brother and his wife, brother and sister. My nephew came home from college for the wedding. He told his friends that his grandparents were getting married. They said, 'Don't you think it's about time?' Dad and Mother Daniels had two wonderful years together. It was like icing on the cake; they both had great marriages before. Then Dad got really sick and we had to put him in a hospital.

"Mother Daniels realized Dad was about to make the transition and she began singing, *When the Roll Is Called Up Yonder, I'll be There*. Dad's lips moved with her until his last breath. Mother Daniel's said, 'Don't you know there's a jubilation on the other side right now!' And I thought, 'You know, I'll just bet there is.' I could see my little Mother up there saying, 'Now, John, you've been there long enough, come on over!' But you see, my Dad died in full consciousness, a whole person. Death was not his enemy; it did not separate him from who he really was. Dad was so much in touch with the physician within him that he died with no fear, in the fullness of his life.

"About eight years ago, I went through a difficult time. I was sued by a patient whose attorney accused me of crucifying his client on a cross of holism. It took seven weeks to resolve the suit in court. I prayed, and had everyone I could think of praying for me. It was a great help. Shortly on the tail of that whole thing, I was called up before the board of Medical Examiners for using castor oil packs on patients. The Cayce readings recommend castor oil packs more than 500 times for eliminations, assimilations, and other therapeutic purposes. In the end, the Chairman of the Board of Medical Examiners said, 'Castor oil packs are under the jurisdiction of Dr. McGarey's homeopathic license, so we can't do anything about it.'

"During this stressful time, my daughter-in-law, who like my son, is a Presbyterian Minister, was a wonderful support to me. She wrote me a letter that I would like to share a part of with you:

'Under his wings, under his wings, who from his love can sever? Under his wings, my soul shall abide, safely abide, forever. Because sometimes the waters wash over us. And they got into the boat, so they could go over to the other side. And Jesus went to sleep on a pillow in the back. Suddenly a storm came up, and the boat began to take on water. And I cried, 'Save me Lord, I am perishing.' And Jesus looked at me with love, and said, 'Peace. Be still.' And the water was still.

'Daughter, why were you so afraid? Do you not believe?'

'Yes Lord, I believe. I was just overcome as the water came up into my boat. I was afraid I would drown. I felt overwhelmed. It was the boat, it was sinking.'

'And Jesus looked at me with love and said, 'Daughter, why were you so afraid? Do you not believe?'

'Oh, yes Lord, I believe.'

'Suddenly I see from deep in my spirit, this was not my boat, and this is not my journey, but the one you, Lord, gave me from my birth. And because you gave it to me, I do completely believe and rest in you.

'And the water was still, and my heart was truly at peace.'

"Months later, I received a letter from the woman seated next to me at Dr. McGarey's lecture. She wrote that the lecture motivated her to reassess her life and values. And she was pleased to have met me, because I rekindled her sense of hope. The lump was down to half its size, so there was progress in her fight against breast cancer. This she attributed mainly to her change in attitude. It gave her courage to end a 13-year relationship draining her of energy and life. She changed her hair style and bought a puppy to love. And she tried some alternative therapies that I had discussed with her, including an herbal remedy for breast cancer prescribed by Hanna Kroeger. In her bra, she wore a high gauss biomagnet over the now-shrinking lump.   She had gone through several three-day fasts and a few colonics. Her choice of foods was healthier, with less fat and more fresh organic fruits and vegetables. As a result of better nutrition and daily exercise, she was becoming trim again. A barter arrangement earned her massages on a weekly basis. And she improved the energy flow in her home by rearranging the furniture and disposing of garments that had bad memories attached to them. These changes made her feel lighter and more in control of her life, which is, in itself, life affirming. She expected the lump to diminish to nothing, which she visualized and prayed for daily. Her letter thanked me for my support and was signed: *'In Christ's Light.'*

•••••••••••••••••

Nothing is stronger than the
human will fortified by faith.

Dr. Gladys Taylor McGarey, MD, MD (H)

•••••••••••••••••

45

•••••••••••••••••

Contact Dr. Gladys Taylor McGarey at:

Scottsdale Holistic Medical Group, P.A.
7350 E. Stetson Drive, Suite 204
Scottsdale, AZ. 85251
Phone: 480-990-1528
Fax: 480-990-3298

•••••••••••••••••

*Know that there is within self a healing
that may be accomplished for the body.*

EDGAR CAYCE
Reading 4021-1

•••••••••••••••••

RECOMMENDED READING

THE PHYSICIAN WITH YOU
Dr. Gladys Taylor McGarey
With Jess Stearn
Health Communications, Inc., 1997

THE STAGES OF STRESS LEADING TO DISEASE
Eileen Bohan Curn and
Dr. Gladys Taylor McGarey
Accord, 1997

DREAMS
Dr. Mark Thurston
St. Martin's Press, 1996

AGELESS BODY, TIMELESS MIND
Dr. Deepak Chopra
Bantam Books, 1997

---

*Each patient carries his own doctor inside him.
They come to us not knowing that truth.
We are at our best when we give the doctor
who resides in each patient a chance to go to work.*

Dr. Albert Schweitzer

5

SOUND HEALING
Interview With Dr. Steven Halpern (Ph.D.)

··················

*Music is the key between
the finite mind and the infinite.*

EDGAR CAYCE
Reading 4098-1 (9)

————————————

*Steven Halpern is a musical magician, a healer with sound. His
music has helped millions experience tranformative moments that
lead to greater wholeness and happiness. Music is one of the
most powerful forces available to humans, and Halpern
wields this medium with immense skill.*

Larry Dossey, MD
Author of: *REINVENTING MEDICINE*
and *HEALING WORDS*

————————————

Steven Halpern, Ph.D. is an internationally acclaimed composer, recording artist, author and educator. His music is specifically composed to support relaxation, wellness and "sound health". He is a passionate advocate for the healing powers of music for spiritual growth, inner peace and world peace. Dr.

48

Halpern produced over 60 recordings in the *Inner Peace* and *Soundwave 2000* subliminal self-improvement series. His music is used throughout the world in hospitals, hospices, holistic healing centers and in homes and businesses.

In recognition of his expertise and contributions to the field of therapeutic music and sound, Dr. Halpern is a member of the Board of Advisors for several leading online health and wellness websites, including wellplace.com. He is also on the advisory board of *Prevention* Magazine. Dr. Halpern was a featured presenter at the Sixth International Conference on Stress, the 1999 and 2000 Conference on Science and Consciousness, the annual Conference of the International Alliance for Accelerated Learning, the American Music Therapy Association, the American Worksite Health Promotion Association and the International Center for Attitudinal Healing.

Dr. Halpern is the recipient of the July, 2000 Music Healing Century Award from the International New Thought Alliance. He presented the keynote speech for the National Conference of the American Massage Therapy Association in September, 2000. He has been a participant in many scientific research studies on the effects of sound on the human body. For more than 30 years, Dr. Halpern has devoted his life to creating healing sounds. They have helped millions of people attain deep relaxation and inner peace.

THE POWER OF SOUND HEALING
Interview With Dr. Steven Halpern

BETTE: Are you familiar with Edgar Cayce's readings on music and sound?

STEVEN: I am. Years ago I read Cayce's Musician's Prayer: *"...let thy prayer ever be...,let me, O God, in my music, in my heart, give that which is as helpfulness to that in the lives of others."* (5265-1 (7), and lights went off in my head. I recognized the words. I knew them. But I didn't know why until later in life. From childhood, I was always seeking more out of music, beyond virtuosity, beyond entertainment. Cayce's readings made me aware that Sound Healing was an age-old art. It existed thousands of years in the Temple Beautiful, in ancient Egypt and in Atlantis. I feel intuitively that I was there then. My purpose in this lifetime is to bring forth healing sounds attuned to the needs of contemporary civilization for the purpose of bringing peace and healing to millions.

BETTE: At what point in history did the healing powers of sound harnessed by ancient cultures subside and then revive?

STEVEN: About 500 years ago the role of music shifted from a religious function in the church to "entertainment". Only recently has the field of Sound Healing reemerged into comprehensive awareness.

BETTE: How did you begin to live out your purpose in this lifetime?

STEVEN: In 1968, at age twenty-two, I was already a classic "Type-A" person experiencing stress-related health challenges. My solution was to find personal inner peace through Sound Healing by combining my training in music and psychology, with insights ranging from ancient shamanic sound traditions to modern bio-physics and vibrational medicine. I began a quest to discover what type of music would be healing in the late 20th century, just as the music of Pythagoras was healing to ancient Greeks or the music of Mozart to 18th century Europeans.

BETTE: What music evolved from your quest?

STEVEN: My discoveries were the basis for my ongoing series of *Inner Peace Music* recordings. After experiencing first-hand the healing powers of music in my own life, I devoted myself to studying, researching and creating healing sounds for the highest good of my listeners. Each album evokes the "Relaxation Response" via sound. Some compositions produce lighter levels of relaxation, and others produce much deeper levels.

BETTE: When you speak about "highest good", are you referring to assisting the listener of your music to connection with God in regard to what they need to enhance that connection?

STEVEN: Yes. The compositions which I have depicted as *Inner Peace Music*, are, as Master Healer Starr Fuentes describes them: *"...music that creates a vibrational field which connects us to Source. That is where the real healing takes place."*

BETTE: Please describe the biological process in the human body when the "Relaxation Response" is evoked via sound.

STEVEN: When an oscillating system like the chakras is stimulated with vibrations of sound, in a way which encourages them to function optimally, healing happens. In my recording *Spectrum Suite*, for example, the background music aligns, attunes and resonates each chakra in an ascending manner. Each keynote is higher than the previous one, like the notes of a scale. These sounds synchronize both hemispheres of the brain, slow down and enhance breathing, and elicit brain wave activity in the deep alpha range. When these traits are induced, a relaxed, peaceful, balanced state of being takes place. This is conducive to connection with Source, a fundamental necessity for healing to take place.

BETTE: Would you say that the body is genetically pre-programmed to heal itself?

STEVEN: It is. Sound Healing can help in the alleviation of a wide range of ailments.

BETTE: There are several methods for correlating sound with color. Do you use any of these modus operandi?

STEVEN: I have found the most useful and universal system of sound and color correlation is the one researched by Dr. Roland Hunt, in England, around 1900. He used 2 seven member scales, the 7 colors of the rainbow and the 7 notes of a major scale. Beginning with the lowest, slowest vibrating member of each, we get: C for red; D for orange; E for yellow; F for green; G for blue; A for indigo; and B for violet. The notes and related colors attune and vibrate their corresponding chakras.

BETTE: Cayce talked about music that could help those suffering from nervous disorders, shell shock, weariness and stress. Are there other disorders that have been alleviated with music?

STEVEN: Scientific research indicates that certain sounds reduce stress, enhance the immune system function, slow down and balance brain wave activity, reduce muscle tension, increase endorphin levels and elicit feelings of love and inner peace. Scientists agree that unrelieved stress is a contributing factor in a wide range of disease such as: hypertension, heart attack, stroke, ulcers, migraine, irritability, inability to concentrate or sleep and sexual dysfunction. But we are not at the point where research maintains that a specific ailment, like cancer, is alleviated by music.

BETTE: Can you relax by doing nothing or just watching television?

STEVEN: People may think they are achieving meaningful relaxation by doing nothing or watching TV, but it is not the level of relaxation which is necessary to balance stress. There are specific deep relaxation techniques that are essential for countering stress. The relaxation-healing connection has been explored in several landmark books like *The Relaxation Response* by Dr. Herbert Benson. He detailed the broad range of bodily functions that work more efficiently when the body is in a state of deep relaxation.

BETTE: Which Sound Healing research projects have you participated in?

STEVEN: Early in my career, I was privileged to work with several leading edge scientists who provided me with a deeper understanding of Sound Healing. With these scientists as my mentors, I conducted Sound Healing studies using brain wave biofeedback, EEG, Kirlian photography and darkfield microscopy which is live blood cell analysis.

BETTE: So Sound Healing is the most efficient way to reduce stress?

STEVEN: It is a very effective way, but not the only way. Sound Healing is a good complement to yoga and meditation. Listening to certain music can bring the body into a deep state of relaxation. But most music is composed for entertainment, dancing or emotional release. It literally makes your nervous system more nervous. There is a time and place for such soundtracks, but reducing stress is never the outcome with that type of music.

BETTE: I understand that the electromagnetic field around the head is effected by sound. Have you researched this?

STEVEN: I used sophisticated equipment to measure the ways subtle energy fields respond to music. In a state of deep relaxation or meditation, the electromagnetic field surrounding the head literally entrains and attunes to the basic electromagnetic field of the earth itself.

BETTE: With what result?

STEVEN: The earth's harmonic resonance has been measured at approximately 8 cycles per second, or 8 Hertz (Hz). The frequency range of the electrical activity of the brain, accessed in states of deep relaxation, is also centered around 8 Hz in deep alpha brain wave patterns. This correspondence is not a coincidence. Just think about how relaxed and rejuvenated we feel when surrounded by nature, in a forest, in the mountains or by the ocean.

BETTE: How do you utilize the earth's harmonic resonance in the creation of your music?

STEVEN: A key component of my composition style is, "Composer, compose thyself." I originate music from my state of being. Before I begin recording in the studio, I get into a deep meditation state, usually by spending time near a lake or in a forest. This gets me "in tune" with the actual vibrational harmonics of the earth's 8 cycle per second resonant frequency. The experience is built into my music. This characteristic makes my recordings different from others.

BETTE: How is your music orchestrated for relaxation?

STEVEN: In *Spectrum Suite* I use the ethereal crystal-clear tones of the electric piano, which creates a sound, I imagine, like a crystal instrument from Atlantean days. Instruments were chosen because their tones are easily accepted into the body. By contrast, the tones of trumpet, oboe and violin are not generally conducive to relaxation. I integrate silence with the sounds of certain instruments. And I use specific qualities of reverberation and echo to stimulate higher-order functioning of the higher senses. *Spectrum Suite* and *Sound Healing* have no hard edges. They are a compilation of the most healing compositions found on all my other albums.

BETTE: How do *Spectrum Suite* and *Sound Healing* compare to classical music in terms of the "Relaxation Response"?

STEVEN: Researchers compared *Spectrum Suite* to the highest rated classical music. In a number of scientific studies, *Spectrum Suite* deeply relaxed over 95% of subjects. The highest rating in classical music was 72%, and that was not a deep relaxation. Mozart rated 65%. These results were contrary to the prevailing attitude that only classical music could be of benefit in relaxing listeners. But the data was, nevertheless, largely ignored.

BETTE: A number of years ago, Georgia Governor Zell Miller announced that every baby born in Georgia would receive a cassette or CD of classical music. This was because Georgia's State Education Commission had ascertained that classical music, like Mozart, has a direct connection to brain development. The Commission said that the *"Mozart Effect"* influenced intelligence in children, specifically in the part of the brain used for math and spacial reasoning. What do you think of this?

STEVEN: Music does effect brain development. Although Governor Zell Miller was well intentioned, he was in error. The term *"Mozart Effect"* is more a tribute to modern myth making and promotional and marketing departments who have pre-empted composers and researchers. I met with Dr. Gordon Shaw, the scientist who did the original research on the *"Mozart Effect"*. He never claimed that *Mozart* made you smarter. In fact, studies show that *Mozart* is less useful than *Spectrum Suite,* which scores higher more often.

BETTE: Then it is far too simplistic a statement to declare that *Mozart* makes you smarter?

STEVEN: Absolutely! Which composition by *Mozart* are we talking about? By which performer? These variables make a huge difference in the effect you experience. The most important consideration is whether a given piece of music works for you. One size does not fit all.

BETTE: When the *"Mozart Effect"* works, for what length of time is the IQ raised?

STEVEN: The *"Mozart Effect"* lasts only 10 - 15 minutes. And *Mozart* should never be played while taking a test. According to Dr. Shaw, it's much too distracting, which is what I have said since 1971.

BETTE: Do you have competitors in the field of Sound Healing?

STEVEN: In the twenty-six years since *Spectrum Suite* brought the concept of the "Relaxation Response" to the public, a number of other recording artists have begun working in this genre. Currently, there are many choices of music to support the healing process.

BETTE: Do people respond to sound because of personal taste?

STEVEN: Yes, but personal taste is only one factor to be considered. The most powerful effect of music is our common physical response to "the beat". The phenomenon known as "rhythm entrainment" describes how an external rhythmic stimulus, such as a ticking clock, drum or pulse in a musical composition, involuntarily causes your heartbeat to match its speed.

BETTE: A fast rhythm produces a fast heartbeat?

STEVEN: It does. There is a subtle response to the *intention* of the musician or composer, a visceral response to the tone of the instruments and an intellectual response to the structure of the composition. In fact, we are culturally conditioned to follow melodic, harmonic and rhythmic patterns in music.

BETTE: Can you explain how we are culturally conditioned to respond to the structure in music, even if we are not trained musicians?

STEVEN: Whether we are conscious of it or not, we automatically mentally analyze what we hear in an attempt to organize sounds into meaningful forms. When we listen to most compositions, we are unconsciously hooked into following the structure and projecting that structure into the future. Let me give you an example: In my workshops, I demonstrate this by singing the first seven notes of the scale: Do-re-mi-fa-so-la-ti; then I pause and do not finish the scale. It is delightful to watch people holding their breath, or hear them actually singing the missing note aloud. They feel too stressed to leave the pattern of notes unfulfilled.

BETTE: Can this approach to tension create relaxation?

STEVEN: Perhaps, but certainly not for many people. Although this is the basis for most Western classical compositions, it is unsuitable, in most cases, for evoking relaxation. There is a basic principle in life that states: "Energy follows thought." If you are paying attention to something outside of you, less energy will be available for internal healing purposes. In my compositions, the listener is never manipulated in this fashion. Instead, as the mind's analytical mode shuts down, the listener is free to be in the "hear and now" with the music.

BETTE: What is "Music of the Spheres" mentioned by Cayce in a number of readings concerning music?

STEVEN: 'Music of the Spheres' refers on one level to actual extremely low frequencies that planets make as they orbit the sun. In order to hear it, we must double the frequency and then double it again, so it can be in the range of physical hearing which is 20 - 20,000 cycles per second. I equate the "Music of the Spheres" to ongoing "broadcasts" of music on "cosmic" radio stations.

BETTE: How does your music relate to this concept?

STEVEN: *Spectrum Suite,* for instance, was already playing in my mind's ear before it materialized into music. I think that is because I heard the "Music of the Spheres" in some manifestation. I have also received other musical visions that resulted in albums like *Ancient Echoes, Higher Ground* and *Gifts of the Angels.*

BETTE: In reading 5401-1, Cayce said: *"For music is of the soul, and one may become mind-soul-sick from music...from certain kinds of music."* Which music can make a person mind-soul-sick?

STEVEN: Just listen to the radio: much rap, some heavy metal, like Judas Priest, most goth, Death Metal, and much techno. For me, being exposed in a restaurant or clothing shop to that mechanical, fast drumbeat, even without the words, or just the sounds, the intention, the lyrics, and the mindset is painful. So I don't stay around long enough to get sick. And let's not forget that Tchaikovsky's *Symphony Pathetique* is known in the annals of music therapy to have caused more depression and suicide than any other music, although they have not tested rock, rap or heavy metal yet.

BETTE: Cayce said that R, O and M are sound vibrations which vibrate to the central forces of the body, and are useful in dissipating undesirable vibrations held fast by a patient's consciousness. Do you use these sound vibrations in your music?

STEVEN: I usually don't use voice in my instrumental music. But there is one major exception. As I was recording *Ancient Echoes* with Georgia Kelly in 1978, much to my surprise, a series of vowels chanted themselves through me. This was recorded as the vocal invocation in that album.

BETTE: Hospital intensive care units, nurseries and operating rooms across the country are playing music for patients because doctors have discovered that it helps a patient's health to improve. In fact, it is so effective, that therapeutic sound is reimbursable under certain conditions of Medicare. I understand that your CDs and tapes are being used in hospitals. What are the results?

STEVEN: They have reported that recovery time after surgery is accelerated, patients experience diminished pain, they call for their nurses less often and ask for less pain medication. My music also helps ease the nurse's stress level.

BETTE: Ancient cultures have used drums, chants, mantras and other sound traditions for healing. Which ancient vibrations have you merged into your music?

STEVEN: The shamanic powers of heartbeat drum, which I use in *Higher Ground*, were honored by ancient cultures. I also utilize the power of vowels and Tibetan healing bowls in *Ancient Echoes*. And my recent recording, *Deja-Blues*, has a wondrous rhythm that always takes me back into a past life.

BETTE: You have also created music to meditate by. How would a meditator use it?

STEVEN: All you need to do is be with the music. Just close your eyes, take a deep breath, and let the music carry you inward. You do not have to concentrate on breathing, stretching, chanting or saying a mantra. Meditation music helps us get in touch with our spiritual nature. In the stillness of meditation we align and attune to the Source where genuine healing takes place.

BETTE: How do you get there?

STEVEN: Through profound relaxation and shifting brain waves into deep alpha and theta. Once the body is relaxed, brain waves become attuned to key frequencies of transcendence, and meditation happens. Many people find it too difficult to deal with meditating in silence. Played softly, my music becomes transparent. Even though the notes are audible, you will often not consciously hear the music. But the vibrations hold the energy field for meditation.

BETTE: What instruments did you use for your meditation music?

STEVEN: I used the grand piano and the electric piano, which is essentially a series of tuning forks. A variety of synthesizers and an assortment of digital samplers was also used. I played the angelic choir with my hands and fingers, rather than directing an actual choir.

BETTE: Is it hard for listeners to get used to non-melodic, non-rhythmic sound that you blend into your compositions?

STEVEN: It's not hard for most listeners. However, if they are highly trained and addicted to classical music, rap and rock, they may have a problem.

BETTE: Do you need headphones to meditate to music?

STEVEN: No. But headphones may provide a deeper experience of internalizing the music as you block out external distractions. If you use headphones, I recommend good ones. I use the Sony Digital V6. They are comfortable and fit around the ear to eliminate outside noises. But once you are in the $50 category most any brand will do.

BETTE: On your website: www.stevenhalpern.com you have tapes for yoga, meditation, relaxation, healing, accelerated learning and subliminal tapes. How do they differ?

STEVEN: Many of the same recordings are suitable for multiple purposes because they help us achieve the fundamental state in which we are in tune with our true self. But some recordings are especially useful for certain outcomes. For example, *Accelerated Learning* incorporates compositions that keeps one alert and in "the learning zone". *Higher Ground*, on the other hand, induces a deeper meditative state and should not be used while driving. Relaxation and balance are keys to helping our human instrument work optimally. Any music that helps us get there will do more than double service.

BETTE: How long have you been producing your subliminal recordings?

STEVEN: I was one of the original pioneers of subliminal self-improvement programs which I have been producing since 1980. Music on the subliminal recordings is chosen from my *Inner Peace* series. Every program features specific suggestions for each topic. I can take the same piece of music and wake you up, or put you to sleep depending on what the subliminal messages are. The subliminal statements are recorded below the threshold of conscious perception. Although you don't hear them, your subconscious mind does, and responds accordingly.

BETTE: You offer an annual award for the most offensive noises emitted by every day appliances and ostensibly healthful devices. Why do you do that?

STEVEN: As an educator, I strive to raise public awareness about noise pollution which is the antithesis of healing via sound. Noise pollution is a social disease - sound dis-healing or sound dis-ease.

BETTE: Who are the recipients of this award?

STEVEN: A *Past Dubious Achievement Award* recipient has been the Sharper Image Ionizer for cars. It was so loud it gave me a pounding headache. The device may have cleaned the air in my car, however, I could not drive while the

Ionizer was in operation. Another "winner" is just about any gas powered leaf-blower because of its soul shattering noise.

BETTE: I have read about your Sound Healing workshops. Where do you teach them?

STEVEN: I offer workshops through organizations like the A.R.E., Unity Church and Science of the Mind Church. My workshops help people get in touch with the power that sound and music can have in their life. I also teach meditation with sound and color. For many years I taught classes all over the country. But from now on I will focus on teaching via the Internet.

BETTE: Any other thoughts that you would like to share?

STEVEN: Honor the power of music in your life. Take time to enjoy "deep listening" at least several times a week. Explore different kinds of music, and listen to your soul. And if we are ever to have peace on our planet, we must first experience peace within ourselves. Find the music that takes you there and enjoy!

•••••••••••••••••

RECOMMENDED READING

TUNING THE HUMAN INSTRUMENT
Dr. Steven Halpern
Spectrum Research Institute, 1977

SOUND HEALTH
Dr. Steven Halpern
Harper & Row, 1985

SOUND, STRESS, AND INNER PEACE
Dr. Steven Halpern
Sound Health Research Institute, 2001

6

COLONICS: THE FULL BODY ENEMA
Joyce Long, Colon Hydrotherapist

....

...for everyone-everybody-should take an internal bath occasionally as well as an external one. They would all be better off if they would.

EDGAR CAYCE
Reading 440-2

It does not take a vivid imagination to extrapolate to our colon from the analogy of what happens to our bodies when we don't shower. While no research has been attempted to validate the importance of colonics, such cleansing makes common sense.

Eric Mein, MD
From: *KEYS TO HEALTH*

Joyce Long has achieved national certification in colon hydrotherapy and massage therapy. She is an instructor, technician/therapist and national and international public speaker. She presents seminars on the importance of colon hydrotherapy and massage to good health. Long serves the Houston medical community, at Joyce Long & Associates Institute, through referrals from medical doctors and Houston hospitals. She utilizes Edgar Cayce's readings and Hanna

Kroeger's alternative health guidance in her colon hydrotherapy and massage practice, and in her everyday life activities. Dedication to her life work has earned Long national recognition in the *International Who's Who*, 1995, and *Woman of the Year - American Biographical Institute*, 1996. She is a member of Compassion In Action (CIA), a hospice group, American Massage Therapy Association (AMTA) and the International Association for Colon Hydrotherapy (I-ACT). The motto at Joyce Long's Wellness Center is: *"We celebrate wellness!"*

Anger causes poisons to be secreted from the glands. Joy has the opposite effect.

EDGAR CAYCE
Reading 281-54

COLONIC CLEANSING
Bette Margolis' Experience

It was my mother's colostomy that propelled me to visit certified colon therapist, Joyce Long. She asked me not to eat or drink carbonated beverages 2 hours before my colonic hydrotherapy session. When I arrived at her office, we talked for a while. I told her how stressed I was concerning my mother's struggle with colon cancer and her colostomy. I feared that, like my mother, I might become one of the millions of people in the USA who develop the disease annually, or one of the 100,000 Americans who have a colostomy each year.

Long said that most people benefit from periodic colonic cleansing except those who suffered from: colon cancer, GI tract, diverticulitis, acute abdominal pain, a recent history of GI bleeding, heart attack or cardiovascular condition, uncontrolled hypertension, general debilitation, vascular aneurysm, seizures, epilepsy, or psychoses.

A full color illustration decorating Long's office wall showed that the colon is a hollow tube-like organ, approximately 5 to 5-1/2 feet long that is made up of muscle structure that moves wastes by peristalsis, a wave-like motion of contraction-relaxation. Long explained that the colon's job is to consistently release wastes.

I asked Long if laxatives or enemas could achieve the same results as colon irrigation. She said they could not because laxatives irritate and stir up the colon. "They cause the body to produce a thin watery substance that goes through the colon." When the inside of the colon is clean, there is more surface area in the colon to absorb water and electrolytes, minerals that are necessary for the human body to maintain itself in stable condition. Healthy peristalsis and regular bowel movements augment the length of time it takes for food to travel through the whole intestine, allowing more nutrients to be absorbed.

Colonic irrigation should be thought of as a complement to regular medical care rather than as the sole treatment for any condition. As part of a comprehensive cleansing, she suggested: occasional fasts, dietary increase in grains, fibers, fruits and vegetables, a decrease in fat and dairy, little or no red meat, no salt, sugar, fried food, alcohol, coffee, tea, or soft drinks that contain caffeine because these beverages dehydrate the stool.

"Cayce said: **"No slop, or those of soft drinks of ANY kind, should be taken..."**, (5545-2 (3) Long said. "Healthy eating includes combinations of food that encourage nutrient absorption, restraint in consumption of mucus-forming foods like bread, milk, and ice cream, and exclusion of foods that cause allergic reactions." She also maintained that there are beneficial effects on the body with: abdominal massage, deep tissue massage or reflexology, saunas to sweat out toxins, lymphatic drainage, deep breathing or an exercise to increase oxygen to the blood and body, drinking 6 to 8 glasses of clean water a day (but not during meal-time because liquids dilute digestive enzymes) to flush the kidneys and lubricate the elimination system, a liver-gallbladder cleanse to rid these organs of impurities, and Atri-Aloe Vera caplets, (can be purchased by calling 1-800-822-6193). "A complete body cleanse should also include yoga and/or meditation," Long said.

I was ready to try my first colonic! But was it going to be embarrassing? Long assured me that her client's dignity was always protected by draping the body, and the procedure was done with modesty for client and technician. She said that I could keep most of my clothing on or remove it and wear a gown. I chose the latter and changed in the bathroom. Then I accompanied Long to the "colonic room", a pleasantly decorated area in the office. It reminded me of a comfortable den with low lighting, upholstered chairs, lamps and attractive artwork on the walls. I was asked to lie on my back on the colonic device, a padded table with an electronically adjustable back rest that supported my knees in the bent position. The table was next to equipment resembling a large cabinet with levers, knobs, pressure gauges, temperature controlled water mixing, back flow prevention valves, pressure and temperature sensors, a built in water purification unit and a lighted glass observation window to view expelled wastes. Long said the colonic device was manufactured with adherence to strict FDA specifications imposing rigorous accountability.

The colonic device had a recessed area, resembling a toilet bowl, just below my hips. It was a receptacle for the rectal nozzle that directed sanitized and filtered water into the colon and then expelled through the plumbing of the colonic equipment. Long handed me a soft pillow for my head, and asked if I wanted to hear relaxing music before she turned on a CD player; I said yes. She used a sterile, disposable, single-use rectal nozzle. It was attached to a tube that was inserted by me into my anus. Long explained that this short insertion does not affect the interior area of the colon; it goes in just past the internal sphincter. A small amount of body temperature water gently flowed into my colon. It stimulated the colon's natural peristaltic action to release softened waste.

Long asked me to inform her if the water was too warm or too cool so she could adjust it. She said that the inflow and release of water with the wastes often takes more time during the first session. This is because the rectum may have to be cleared of heavily impacted wastes before the intestine can be filled and peristalsis stimulated. Nervousness at a first colonic session is another reason that peristalsis may shut down. The length of time for a colonic varies according to individual need and response. My first colonic took 45 minutes. During that time, Long periodically did hand and foot reflexology on me. She also placed a heating pad on my abdomen to help activate the colon to release. At the same time, she reminded me to breathe deeply, suggesting imagery for relaxation. In addition, Long meditated with me to help my body, mind and spirit relax. Occasionally, she left the room when I needed privacy. Then she returned when I called her through an intercom, because I needed the water temperature adjusted or felt some mild cramping. Every now and then I looked at the observation window and was amazed to view all the accumulated wastes irrigating out of my colon. While water evacuated from my colon, Long gave me an abdominal massage in specific patterns to help me eliminate considerable amounts of gas.

When the colonic was completed, I followed Long's instructions. I went to the bathroom and sat on the toilet for a while, with my feet on a stool and my back up against the rear of the toilet. Wastes continued to eliminate sporadically for a brief time. Before I left her office, Long told me that it was important to drink plenty of water to bathe my organs and the trillions of cells in my body. She also said to drink juices and herbal teas for tissue hydration. Equally important was nourishing my body with good quality organic food containing sodium, potassium and magnesium, so the electrolyte level of the colon would naturally replenish itself. For 24 hours after the procedure I ate pureed soup, as Long had suggested. I followed the rule to avoid raw vegetables for 2 days, reduce meat consumption for 3 days, and not to consume shellfish, sushi, MSG or any carbonated products.

Except for mild cramping during the session, I found colon hydrotherapy to be a relatively comfortable and safe experience. I left Long's office with a heightened sense of mental clarity, feeling profoundly purified, light and vital. In the days that followed I made changes in my diet and lifestyle, according to Long's recommendations. This included proper rest so my body could recuperate and rejuvenate. My problems with constipation disappeared, and I continued to feel energetic and experience mental alertness. My skin and eyes were clearer and I maintained a feeling of good health, relaxation and well-being. I am scheduled for another colonic irrigation 10 days from my first session. I will continue the procedure every 10 days until all the waste is flushed out of my colon. If needed, I will repeat colonic irrigation every 3 to 6 months thereafter.

•••••••••••••••••

*Colonic irrigations are recommended (by Cayce) to improve
the elimination's of "poisons" and thus relieve the strain on the
heart; these are to be given "professionally and scientifically'"
with great care to ensure a strain is not placed on the heart...;
to be given in a series spaced 10 days apart until all the mucus
is gone from the rinse waters - this goal is to be accomplished
gradually and not attempted in just one or two treatments; the
water is to be at body temperature with a level tablespoon of salt
and a level teaspoon of soda added to each gallon of water; the
final rinse waters are to contain Glyco-Thymoline.*

ERIC MEIN, MD
From: *KEYS TO HEALTH*

••••••••••••••••

RECOMMENDED READING

EDGAR CAYCE'S GUIDE TO COLON CARE:
The First Step To Vibrant Health
Sandra Duggan, RN,
A.R.E. Press, 1995

PERFECT DIGESTION
Deepak Chopra
Harmony Books, 1995

Contact Joyce Long at:

Joyce E. Long Wellness Center
1308 James Street
Rosenberg, TX 77471
Phone: 713-623-0866

7

MEDITATION AND NEUROTHERAPY
Dr. Nancy E. White (Ph.D.)

....

*Meditation is listening to the Divine within. It is not musing,
not daydreaming; but, as...your bodies (are) made up of the
physical, mental and spiritual, it is the attuning of the mental
body and the physical body, to its spiritual source.*

EDGAR CAYCE
Reading 281-41 (8)

———————————

*As we discharge negative emotions and
rigidly held beliefs from our past woundings,
neurochemistry seems to be altered, brain waves
are normalized, the ability to move from state
to state is enhanced and our psyche alters.*

Nancy E. White, Ph.D.
From: *THE JOURNAL OF MIND TECHNOLOGY
AND OPTIMAL PERFORMANCE,* 1993

———————————

Nancy E. White, Ph.D. is a licensed psychologist, professional marriage and family therapist, chemical dependency specialist, compulsive gambling counselor, and a registered Neurotherapy practitioner in clinical practice for over 25 years. She is President and Clinical Director of the Neurotherapy Center and Clinical Director of The Enhancement Institute, Houston, Texas. Dr. White is a pioneer practitioner in the use of EEG Neurotherapy, an advanced form of biofeedback. She is listed in *Who's Who in American Women*: 14th, 15th, 16th, 17th, 18th, 19th Editions, *Notable Women of Texas,* 1st Edition, *Who's Who in the World,* 11th and 12th Edition, and in *Who's Who in Medicine and Health Care*: 1st. Edition.

MEDITATION AND NEUROTHERAPY
Insights By Nancy E. White, Ph.D.

Meditation, derived from the Latin word *Meditari,* means "to heal." It involves neither religious nor cultural beliefs. Meditators learn to transcend the material world in an effortless process that quiets the thinking mind, taking it to a state of silence, a place of no-thing-ness that Eastern religions talk about. In the peaceful flow of altered consciousness, a state of heightened awareness of the infinite Divine may arise within the meditator. Dissolving into God by means of meditation is said to waken the soul. In the meditative state, the focal point of control shifts from the external world to an internal one, allowing us to encounter our true selves in peace and freedom from judgment embedded in our higher nature.

During the 70s and 80s a considerable number of studies from several countries documented calculable physical changes occurring in the body during meditation. Research validated claims that meditators enrich their lives by activating a healing quality of rest which aided in reducing anxiety, depression and deeply rooted stress and trauma stored in the body.

Dr. Nancy White, whose interview provided background for this chapter, has been meditating for over 30 years. She initially became interested in meditation as a form of relaxation, starting out by using taped sounds of specific frequencies that took her into a fairly deep state. But she quickly came to believe that the greatest healing comes from being able to meditate without external feedback because nothing is influencing you that does not originate from within you. Dr. White said that she can eliminate the mind chatter most people live with and abide in quietness of mind without the fault-finding or judgments most people inflict upon themselves. "Like anyone else, I can get upset by external circumstances, but I seem to be less reactive than most of the people I know and remain peaceful inside most of the time," she said. "Neurotherapy, also known as EEG Neurofeedback Therapy, has enhanced meditation capability for me."

She explained that Neurotherapy, a non-invasive treatment protocol involving no drugs, assists an individual, with state of the art computerized instruments, or EEG, to encourage the brain to enter and maintain itself in a so-called theta state. This is a very deep meditative state just above sleep that ordinarily could not be held very long by anyone but an advanced meditator. "It has been said that the Zen Master concluded that with alpha-theta Neurotherapy, one can attain in less than two months what it would take a Zen meditator to do in twenty years," said Dr. White.

User friendly Neurotherapy, a sophisticated cousin to biofeedback, induces a deep meditative state similar to the way we feel when we are lying in bed neither asleep nor awake, aware but not thinking. Going that deep bypasses the resistance of waking ego, enabling an individual to confront emotional pain with composure. In this state, one is empowered to understand why the emotional pain was taken on. When this realization occurs, it implements release of the painful emotions, and subsequent healing can take place so the individual can recover and live from more of his/her true nature.

"Most of our deep psychological woundings come from unskilled perceptions and adaptations that we form during early childhood," Dr. White explained. "We all end up with some woundings whether we were abused or not." She said that when we are small and helpless, dependent beings in a world of powerful giants called adults, we may perceive certain actions and events as frightening or dangerous, which, as adults, we probably would shrug off. These early childhood fears and perceptions are stored in specific areas of the brain as survival material. But as we age, this information becomes inaccessible to us in the waking state, because our predominant brain wave frequency speeds up as we get older.

For example, when we are infants our predominant brain wave frequency is very slow, roughly four cycles or less per second, which is one reason babies sleep so much. A toddler's brain waves are a little faster, predominantly "theta" or about 4 to 8 cycles per second. By the time we become teenagers the predominant brain wave frequency is much higher, in the ranges we call "alpha", which is a quiet, alert state ranging from about 8 to 12 cycles per second. This is the state we are usually in when we people-watch at the mall. "Students of advanced Zen, yoga and other forms of meditation nurturing inner awareness, display ability to produce high amplitude, low frequency, stable "alpha" and "theta" activity," Dr. White said.

"Beta" is a frequency range of greater than 13 cycles per second in which the ego is most active. We use "beta" for active thinking and solving problems. While the ego is a critical part of our personality, it has some quirks. It dislikes change, relishes security and enforces the status quo. "Even if we are miserable, the ego may seem satisfied if only because certainty indicates survival," Dr. White said. "It seems as though we live in a tug of war between our higher selves and the ego, with the higher self yearning for growth and self-development, while the ego pulls back from the unknown."

The alpha-theta neurofeedback protocol enhances the ability to revert to the low arousal, predominantly the theta brain wave state we were in as toddlers and small children. In that state we find it easier to retrieve and release early traumas and memories from the unconscious mind without interference from the ego. Frequently we find resources we did not know we possessed. When an adult's past traumas rise to consciousness during an alpha-theta meditative session, the mature person sitting in the chair becomes the resource-self who can add a more seasoned perspective to the situation. He/she can even enter into a flashback and rescue the violated child-self. Individuals frequently come out of a single alpha-theta meditative session feeling less of a victim in life because they have found resources dormant within themselves that they were neither aware of nor had owned before.

Controlled studies support the clinical use of alpha-theta Neurotherapy to help individuals recover from addictions, depression, anxiety and other mood disturbances, and the emotional consequences of major life events and losses (also known as post-traumatic stress). A companion protocol has been found effective in resolving the symptoms of Attention Deficit Disorder (ADD and ADHD) and certain closed head injuries (TBI).

Neurotherapy has helped to improve the lives of persons with normal brain function as well. Executives, professionals, athletes, artists, writers, musicians and individuals from many other walks of life have found that Neurotherapy enhances their creativity, productivity and performance, and helps them acquire greater peace of mind, optimism and awareness of their spiritual nature.

Some practitioners have witnessed profound changes resulting from Neurotherapy. Several years ago Gary Schummer, Ph.D. treated a group of AIDS patients with the alpha-theta neurofeedback protocol. After two-and-a-half months of treatment, testing showed an average increase of thirty-four-percent in T-cell count.

Dr. White recalled a young man she and her colleagues worked with sometime ago. He dropped out of college and was on total disability because he suffered from panic disorder and Epstein-Barr syndrome. "About two-thirds of the way through his alpha-theta neurofeedback program the young man reached a state of homeostasis," she said. "Apparently his immune system was getting stronger, because he was getting healthier. By the end of his treatment both the panic disorder and the Epstein-Barr syndrome had disappeared."

A woman addicted to drugs, who had been raped when she was twelve years old, was treated by Dr. White with the Neurotherapy protocol. While in a deep meditation state, during one alpha-theta neurofeedback session, the woman actually saw the face of her rapist in front of her. Because she did not experience the strong fear and emotional reaction her ego might have had in the waking state, she was able, as the twelve year old, to order the rapist to leave her alone and never bother her again. The success of this confrontation caused a shift in her unconscious survival material, reflected in brain wave activity and in its underlying neurochemistry. She lost her craving for drugs, because she resolved the effects of her abuse, which was the core issue underlying her addiction.

By promoting positive personality changes in addicted individuals, the alpha-theta neurofeedback therapy may help prevent future relapses. Even after an individual stops using, he or she may continue to be unhappy and dysfunctional if underlying maladaptive personality disorders remain unaddressed. Many studies have shown that sustained prevention of relapse requires that both the craving behavior and the underlying psychological disorders be addressed.

Alpha-theta neurofeedback therapy involves attaching small electrodes to specific points on the scalp. The eletrodes perform the same listening function as a physician's stethoscope, sending the faint signals they pick up to a computerized electroencephalograph, or EEG. The signals are analyzed and compared with the specific program the therapist has set up for the individual. When the signals and the program match, the computer gives the brain a reward in the form of pleasing musical tones, encouraging it to do more of the same. The therapist can monitor the individual's brain wave activity and training progress by means of graphs and statistics that appear on the computer screen. A printout preserves the history of each session for review and assessment of overall progress.

71

Before beginning a program of Neurotherapy, a trained therapist works with the individual to clarify the outcome he/she would achieve. An image or a scenario of the desired outcome is worked out (i.e. a scene in which the person intensely experiences him/herself being completely at ease in a formerly anxiety-producing situation) and verbalized to the person at the beginning of each session as he/she relaxes into the deep meditative state that characterizes "theta" predominance. In this state, limitless possibility exists because the skepticism of waking ego is absent and because the unconscious tends to accept imagined information as real, especially if the theme is repeated again and again with desire and feeling. Alpha-theta Neurotherapy enhances actualization of the desired outcome by just such frequent reinforcement. The protocol calls for approximately 30 sessions scheduled at least four or five times a week over a 6-to-8 week period. In cases of severe addiction or debilitating dysfunction a person may start with as many as 2 sessions a day for an initial period.

At the end of the alpha-theta protocol, many persons who continue to practice find it possible to enter that deep meditative state without the EEG feedback. Without the machinery you would sit comfortably, close your eyes and focus on your breathing. "You could vocalize a mantra such as 'om' or 'I am,' practice anything that enhances focus, or you could just completely let go and watch thoughts float by without holding on to them," Dr. White suggested. "Another excellent means is to meditate according to Edgar Cayce's readings." (See description of the Edgar Cayce meditation procedure on following pages.) Dr. White pointed out that whatever method you choose to move into a deep meditative state, independent of external feedback, you will find that the alpha-theta Neurotherapy protocol experience allows you to get there quicker and with more ease.

••••••••••••••••

Alpha-theta neurofeedback may eventually allow humanity to transcend our present limited consciousness as we experience true liberation from automatic stress responses, addiction, chronic pain, anxiety, depression, and a variety of other cognitive, emotional and physical limitations.

Nancy E. White, Ph.D.
From: *THE JOURNAL OF MIND TECHNOLOGY AND OPTIMAL PERFORMANCE*, 1993

•••••••••••••••

There are more than 1000 Neurotherapy practitioners in the USA. Dr. White is the treasurer of the Society for the Study of Neuronal Regulation (SSNR).

For further information contact Dr. White at:

The Enhancement Institute
4600 Post Oak Place
Suite 301
Houston, TX. 77027
713-552-0091

•••••••••••••••

EDGAR CAYCE MEDITATION PROCEDURE

Meditation is a lifestyle profoundly influenced by our ideals, purposes, thoughts and nutrition. Assuming that you are consciously working with these continual influences, the following meditation procedures are recommended:

1. Set a regular time to meditate. Time consistency ensures the likelihood that you will remember to meditate. It also may assist you in attaining a focus quickly. Choose a time of day when you will be least distracted, alert and able to maintain a focus on your spiritual aspirations and ideals.

2. To create the right mood for centering on your spiritual aspirations, choose from among the many aids for attunement. Some suggestions are:

    a) Reading from the Bible or other spiritual literature;

    b) Conscious focused breathing;

    c) Gentle head exercises to relax tense neck and shoulders. Slowly rotate head forward, then backward, then side to side, circle one way and then the other;

    d) Chanting;

    e) Use incense;

    f) Listen to inspirational, or quieting, centering music.

3. Pray. Attune your mind through prayer for a few minutes. There is a difference between prayer and meditation. Cayce said, *"Prayer is like talking to God. Meditation is like listening to God."* (2946-6 (5). You may wish to recite the Lord's Prayer or another prayer which can be said silently or aloud. There are many forms of prayer: petitionary, praise, thanksgiving and forgiveness. Each day select an appropriate type of prayer.

4. Choose an affirmation, memorize it and recite it several times. Begin by saying the affirmation aloud, then repeat it silently. Each lesson in the book *A Search For God*, offers a Cayce reading with a specific meditation affirmation keyed to the chapter's concepts of spiritual growth. If the affirmation seems too lengthy, repeat only a line or a phrase most meaningful to you. Actual meditation begins when you start feeling the meaning of the words. At that point it is unnecessary to repeat the affirmation. Instead, silently hold the spirit of the feeling in your attention. All meditators experience wandering attention seconds into their meditation (alpha-theta Neurotherapy eliminates or reduces wandering attention). Gently bring your attention back by silently repeating the affirmation once or twice. When you resume feeling the meaning and spirit behind the words, release the affirmation and hold the feeling in silence. You will probably have to do this many times during the meditation, if you have not been prepared with the alpha-theta Neurotherapy protocol, because the mind is accustomed to darting from thought to thought. Don't be discouraged! Despite the frequency of internal and external distractions, even short periods of quieting your mind can produce positive effects on your body, mind, emotions and spirit.

5. When your meditation is over, pray for others for several minutes. You may wish to pray for someone who requested that you pray for their healing or a change in the conditions of their life. Or, pray for those you have concern for by blessing them with the words, "God's will be done."

•••••••••••••••••

The body, mind and soul are interconnected in such a
way that certain actions will automatically lead to
'the magic silence' and the awakening of our better selves.

EDGAR CAYCE
Reading 137-3

•••••••••••••••••

·················

RECOMMENDED READING

GOD CALLING
A.J. Russell
Berkeley Publishing Group, February, 2002

MEDITATION:
Gateway To Light
Elsie Sechrist
A.R.E. Press, 1990

MEDITATION AND THE MIND OF MAN
Mark Thurston, Ph.D. and Herbert Puryear
A.R.E. Press, 1975

(Audio Tape)
EDGAR CAYCE MEDITATION
Mark Thurston, Ph.D.
A.R.E. Press, 1990

8

Part 1
COLOR THERAPY - COLOUR ENERGY
Susanne Murphy, Colour Therapist

Part 2
ESOGETIC COLORPUNCTURE
ACU-LIGHT THERAPY
Manohar Croke, Colorpuncture Therapist
and Kirlian Energy Emission Analyst

••••••••••••••••

...the body mentally - and the body
in its nerve reaction - would respond
as quickly to color forces as it
would to medicinal properties...

Edgar Cayce
Reading 4501-1

_____

All bodies radiate those vibrations with which it,
the body, controls itself in mental, in physical,
and such radiation is called the aura.

Edgar Cayce
Reading 5756-1

•••••••••••••••••

Inger Naess is the founder of Colour Energy Corporation which began in 1988. She resides in Norway and teaches about color energy throughout Europe. For many years Naess studied the effects of color on the human body and psyche while working in various professions: kindergarten teacher, fashion, interior designer, import/export entrepreneur and gallery owner. Her passion for color led her to experiment with its influence in water. Her discoveries evolved into the development of a line of personal care products based on the science and philosophy of color therapy. Naess is the author of *Colour Energy* and other books on the subject of color application.

...the body's chemistry is responsive to our thoughts
and feelings. Thoughts actually affect a chemical change.
Visualizing and breathing color is a mental and emotional
way of activating chemical changes in the body.

Deepak Chopra
From: *HEALTH NATURALLY*
(For a magazine article,)
August/September, 1995

Susanne Murphy, Director of Colour Energy Corporation, is a graphic artist, certified Colour Therapist, member of the International Association of Colour Therapy, London, England, and an Instructor with the International Colour Energy Educational Systems. Murphy has appeared on numerous television shows including a series about complementary medicine on the Life Channel, and on Healthy Homes which aired on the Discovery Network.

Part 1

COLOUR ENERGY
The Whole Life Expo

This year's Whole Life Expo in Denver, Colorado was holistic heaven! Experts in various alternative health care professions offered informative lectures, workshops and samples of their services. There was a wonderful array of interesting booths exhibiting a variety of remedies, therapeutic devices, salves, scents, stones and crystals, spiritual art work, New Age CDs and cassettes and readings by gifted psychics.

I was attracted to a table with a bright yellow banner. It was decorated with an illustration of the sun radiating rainbow colors that umbrellaed a sign with the words: *Colour Energy, For Body And Soul.* On display was a line of goods including: essential oils to energize the chakras (our seven main psycho-spiritual energy centers located along the spine), colorful chakra jewelry to help align and balance the energy centers of the body, a chakra gemstone necklace, a chakra gemstone kit with seven polished gemstones correlating to our seven main chakra centers. and a booklet about the healing power of each gemstone. There were soap bars with delicious scents, liquid soaps and shower gels in the seven colors of the visible light spectrum. And there were books on how one's innate colors are linked to personality, sex life, health issues, and even one's profession, money and success. An interesting array of CDs was exhibited. They were designed to balance the chakras with sounds corresponding to musical scales harmonizing perfectly with primary and secondary chakra related colors. And there were tests to identify one's color strengths and weaknesses for the purpose of finding the correct color energy to balance one's chakras.

I read the literature on the table about the Aurastar 2000, an advanced European biofeedback imaging system distributed by Colour Energy Corporation. The concept of the apparatus is based on the ancient art of Ayurvedic medicine, the science of biofeedback, reflexology, kinesiology, neural therapy, vibrational frequencies and also the suggestions in the Edgar Cayce readings on how to create a *"...mechanical device to determine not only the aura of individuals but [for] the diagnosis of disorders in various portions of the body..."* (0040-006).

For most people the aura or human energy field around the body cannot be seen by the naked eye. But with the Aurastar 2000 equipment, a picture of one's aura can be viewed on screen. This feat is accomplished by placing the hand on the Aurastar's sensor which reads the energy that is emitted through the reflex points on the hand. The vibrational information is then transferred and translated to a computer program displaying the bioenergetic color data of one's aura onto a full body color picture on Aurastar's computer monitor. A trained aura counselor can analyze the aura's representation and interpret its colors in terms of a physical and emotional adequacy, or deficiency of the body at the specific moment of definition.

Colour Bath, the main Colour Energy Corporation product, is a non-toxic, natural organic pigment available in the seven visible colors of the light spectrum. Each color is packaged in recyclable paper envelopes or plastic containers. Added to one's bath water, the colors are intended to awaken vital body energies. Colour Energy Corporation vouches for Colour Bath's safety, claiming that it can be used by people of all ages with sensitive skin or allergies. It contains no animal byproducts, metals, chemicals, coal or petroleum. The coloring material, combined with filtered water and glycerin, contains organic European Union (EU) approved colors made from the organic elements of oxygen, hydrogen, nitrogen and carbon. European Union standards are more rigid than America's FDA's which sanction FD&C coloring as North America's main color agent, even though testing is not conclusive. FD&C colors are chemically derived, stain the skin and are absorbed by the body. Murphy believes that ingesting chemical agents pollutes the body, and eventually causes hazardous health effects over a lifetime of use.

"Why bathe in color?" I asked Susanne Murphy, director of the company. Murphy stated that healers, spiritual teachers and many scientists, including those at the National Institute of Mental Health and the Endocrine Laboratory at Massachusetts Institute of Technology, agree that the body absorbs the vibration that color gives off. It triggers hormone production which influences our entire complex biochemical system and affects our physical, mental, emotional and spiritual health.

Body organs, body systems and psychological equilibrium are related to our seven major chakras, the main energy ductless glandular centers that are part of every person. Each chakra is governed by one of seven visible color energies: red, orange, yellow, green, blue, indigo and violet. When the body is out of balance even slightly, we feel the effects on a physical, mental, emotional and/or spiritual level. Factors like improper diet, lack of exercise and/or stress are the main culprits responsible for body imbalances. But lifestyle changes and the utilization of the color that can help reenergize the chakras, will help restore and maintain good health.

The color spectrum evolves from light, our most significant source of energy. Light embraces all wavelengths of the electromagnetic spectrum of colors. And each visible color in the light spectrum contains a specific wavelength and frequency responsible for producing a particular energy and nutritive effect. Our chakras absorb what they need in the light spectrum, to energize themselves in the particular wavelength of their elemental color, and then pass the remainder on to other glands.

It is important to understand the power of color, and the chakras they are associated with, in order to use color energy effectively. For example, the vital and very passionate color red, which is the intrinsic pigment of the root chakra, is the life force that invigorates our body. It gives us physical and inner strength, security, vitality and will-power needed for endurance, aggressiveness, survival instincts, connection to the earth and the knowledge that we exist. Red energy helps fight colds and stimulates the circulatory system especially when we have cold hands or feet. In the old days, farmers ate beet soup as a source of red energy high in iron which gave them strength to do hard labor. Today, scientific tests have proven that the color red will increase heartbeat, blood pressure and body temperature. People suffering from heart trouble, high blood pressure or difficulty in stabilizing body temperature will instinctively avoid the color red.

"Color energy is one of many ways to encourage and maintain good health," Murphy explained. She pointed out that we can nurture our health by choosing specific colors in certain food, herbs, seasonings, oils, clothing, furnishings, general surroundings and gemstones, as well as the color we add to our bath water. "Bathing in color is a very effective way to reap the vibratory benefits of color energy," Murphy said. Red energy, for example, is found in many foods such as tomatoes - known to help prevent prostate cancer - strawberries and cherries. Gemstones of ruby and red tiger's eye also contain red energy, and so do the oils of ylang ylang and sandalwood. Juniper, cinnamon and vetiver are other sources of red food vibrational energy that can boost vitality. The herbal correlation with red energy is: ginseng, echinacea, cayenne pepper, iron, goldenseal and ginger.

Using color vibrational frequencies to heal the body, mind, emotions and spirit is well documented by ancient civilizations in Egypt, India, Arabia, Greece and also in native American cultures. Color Therapy has recently resurfaced as a powerful healing technique. Today, many alternative health care practitioners and trained color therapists routinely use color to heal a variety of disorders. "Analyzing our reactions to color can tell us a great deal about ourselves and how we use or need to use energy," Murphy said.

Before her association with Colour Energy, Murphy said that she had bouts with frequent digestive and constipation problems which often lasted up to five days. Her symptoms included avoidance of the color yellow in her diet and wardrobe and an allergy to rosemary oil, a digestive stimulant known to expand the energy of the upper digestive system and mental abilities. Shortly after Murphy became acquainted with Colour Energy, she decided to try adding yellow Colour Bath to her bath water. At first she could not use the whole package because it was too intense to experience the full effects of yellow. According to her Aurastar aura picture, yellow energy was overabundant in her mental aura, but lacking in her physical aura. It is important to understand that the chakra system governs mental, physical, emotional and spiritual aspects of a person's well-being. This knowledge is fundamental in the proper direction of the correct color energy to the chakras that require a boost for balanced functioning. "My difficulty was that my yellow energy was being consumed by my overactive mental demands. This affected my upper digestive system which was not receiving the yellow energy it needed to function properly," Murphy explained.

When she immersed herself in the tinted yellow bath water, she visualized the color being transmitted into her body. Yellow is the innate color of the solar plexus chakra. Within ten minutes of bathing in yellow water, her solar plexus pulsated strongly because her body was absorbing yellow energy, and working its power to bring in vibrational frequencies that she lacked. It took a month of bathing in gradually stronger strengths of yellow before she was able to use full strength yellow Colour Bath without feeling overwhelmed. Then she continued bathing in full strength yellow for months. She also added more yellow foods to her diet, wore yellow clothing and meditated on the color yellow. Subsequently, she found that her allergy to rosemary oil, which has a similar vibration to yellow, disappeared along with her constipation problems. Her mood, energy level and feeling of general well-being improved and so did her memory. "Improving one's memory is generally related to stimulating the yellow solar plexus chakra," Murphy said.

Colour Energy confirms Cayce's readings about mind being the builder of good or bad health. Thoughts are things which can cause illness by negative thinking, conditions and activities. "Color vibrational energy can reach each chakra in pure form only if the right mental attitude is present. The chakras receive color vibrations in the same state of distorted vibrational imbalance as negative mental activity," Murphy stated.

Colour Energy Corporation offers an international correspondence school to the public. It dedicates itself to educating people on using color for reinforcing or redirecting their energy for vigorous physical, mental and emotional health and vibrant expression of the soul-self.

Information about classes and
Colour Energy products is on website:

www.colourschool.com, and
www.colourenergy.com

••••••••••••••••

The shortest wavelength of electromagnetic radiation (light),
to which we have given the name "violet", is associated
with the pituitary gland by the Cayce readings.

Roger Lewis
From: *COLOR AND THE*
EDGAR CAYCE READINGS

•••••••••••••••

POSTSCRIPT BY AUTHOR

My favorite color is violet, the color of inspiration, creativity and of giving to others. Violet is the vibration of our top chakra, the crown center. It is the color that reflects the state and power of knowingness and spiritual connection. Violet is the energy of our belief system focused on working for a higher purpose. Universal energy is accessed with violet. It gives creative vibrational flow for fresh ideas that nourish artistic talent and inspiration. A positive violet energy makes things happen. This calming color is also known to help insomnia, headaches and eczema. Violet is also an anti-bacterial cleanser for skin rashes or burns. Its energy is in lavender, jasmine and magnolia essential oils, valerian, vervain and meadowsweet herbs, eggplant, plums, kale, broccoli and purple grapes. Amethyst and quartz crystal contain ideal violet vibrational energies to be surrounded with when meditating and are related to higher energy that opens us to the heavens, our higher self and to God.

I tried a packet of full strength violet Colour Bath in my bath water. At first, its full intensity was a mild shock to behold. But as I bathed in the concentrated violet waters, its color quickly became wonderfully relaxing. My high stress day and matching headache disappeared within 5 minutes of soaking in violet Colour Bath. Afterwards, I felt sufficiently at ease, motivated and focused to work on this chapter about color energy.

83

*The history of healing with color is extensive and
the results are so convincing that the natural conclusion
is that all healing should begin and end with color.*

From: *ISSUES*
December, 1993/January, 1994

••••••••••••••••

COLOUR ENERGY REFERENCE CHART

Light coming through our eyes stimulates the pituitary gland, which can be compared to the master switch of all the glands in our body. The entire spectrum of colors is derived from light. It is the function of the pituitary gland to send signals from all the colors in light by splitting the color wavelengths and sending the right signal to the correct gland. The glands are connected to one of seven major chakras existing in every person. Each chakra is guided by one of seven corresponding colors.

Colour Bath offers seven colors that correspond to the seven major chakras in the human body. Turquoise and pink were also added because of their unique high vibrational healing benefits.

RED: Root Chakra. Encourages vitality, courage, self confidence. Red is the grounding color connecting us to our physical self. Ylang Ylang or Sandalwood Oil are recommended as compatible choices for adding to red Colour Bath because their frequency/wavelength is similar to the color red.

ORANGE: Spleen Chakra. Joins us to our emotional self, happiness, confidence, restfulness. Orange brings joy to our workday and strengthens our appetite for life. Melissa or Orange Oil are recommended as compatible choices for adding to orange Colour Bath because their frequency/wavelength is similar to the color orange.

YELLOW: Solar Plexus Chakra. Tied to our mental self, wisdom, clarity, self-esteem. Yellow energy is brain food that stimulates interest and curiosity. Rosemary or Bergamont Oil are recommended as compatible choices for adding to yellow Colour Bath because their frequency/wavelength is similar to the color yellow.

GREEN: Heart Chakra. United to unconditional love, balance, self control. Helps relax muscles, nerves and thoughts. Cleanses our energy giving peace, harmony and renewal. Eucalyptus and Pine Oil are recommended as compatible choices for adding to green Colour Bath because of their similarity to the color green in frequency/wavelength.

BLUE: Throat Chakra. Fosters a connection to holistic thought, general health, knowledge, hormonal balancer, and is a mentally relaxing color ideal for sleep problems, stress, or hyper-active children. Geranium or Chamomile oil are recommended as compatible choices for adding to blue Colour Bath because their frequency/wavelength is similar to the color blue.

INDIGO: Brow Chakra. Cultivates a union with our unconscious self, intuition, mysticism, understanding, imagination, psychic powers and increases dream activity. Patchouli or Frankincense Oil are recommended as compatible choices for adding to indigo Colour Bath because their frequency/wavelength is similar to the color indigo.

VIOLET: Crown Chakra. Links us to our spiritual self, beauty, creativity, inspiration. Violet purifies our thoughts and feelings, enhancing artistic talent and ideals. Violet stimulates the pituitary gland. Lavender or Jasmine oil are recommended as compatible choices for adding to violet Colour Bath because their frequency/wavelength is similar to the color violet.

TURQUOISE: Thymus Chakra. Bolsters confidence, self-expression and strengthening concentration and control over speech, boosts the immune system. Tea Tree or Clary Sage Oil are recommended as compatible choices for adding to turquoise Colour Bath because their frequency/wavelength is similar to the color turquoise.

PINK: Heart Chakra. Nourishes universal love, kindness, consideration and helps remove all unwanted aggression and irritation, giving peace of mind. Rose or Rosewood Oil are recommended as compatible choices for adding to Pink Colour Bath because their frequency/wavelength is similar to the color pink.

RECOMMENDED READING

COLOR AND THE EDGAR CAYCE READINGS
Roger Lewis
Edgar Cayce Foundation, 1973

COLOUR ENERGY
Inger Naess
Colour Energy Corporation, 1996

———————————

Colour Energy's products are sold in over 1500
Health and New Age stores throughout the world.

For information contact:

COLOUR ENERGY CORPORATION
758 Powell Street
Vancouver, British Columbia, Canada V6A 1H6
Toll Free: 1-800-225-1226
Phone: 604-687-3757
Fax: 604-687-3758
Website: www.colourenergy.com
email: colour@colourenergy.com

•••••••••••••••

Part 2

ESOGETIC COLORPUNCTURE
ACU-LIGHT THERAPY
Interview With Manohar Croke

••••••••••••••••••

*...man is essentially a being of light, and the modern science of
photobiology is presently proving this. In terms of healing, the
implications are immense. We now know, for example, that light
can initiate, or arrest cascade-like reactions in the cells, and genetic
cellular damage can be repaired within hours by faint beams of light.*

Dr. Fritz Albert Popp,
Biophysicist

Manohar Croke, CCP, BA (Psychology) is a certified practitioner of
Esogetic Colorpuncture and a Kirlian Energy Emission Analyst, trained at the
International Mandel Institute, Zurich. For over eleven years she studied with
Peter Mandel, originator of Esogetic Colorpuncture. Her education is a
continuing work in progress to keep abreast of Mandel's newly developed color
therapies which she offers to clients. Croke has conducted extensive research in
Kirlian photography and color therapy. Her numerous articles on the subject
have been published nationwide in journals, magazines and books such as
American Journal of Acupuncture, *Light Years Ahead*, and *Spirit of Change*
Magazine. Croke also trained in Hakomi Trauma Therapy (somatic
psychotherapy techniques for processing trauma held in the body and nervous
system.) For the past 7 years she has trained in the Diamondlogos method of
spiritual therapy. She integrates her knowledge of these systems into her unique
approach of the application of Colorpuncture Therapy. Croke's Colorpuncture
and Kirlian Energy Emission Analysis workshops are offered nationwide. She
practices at the Institute for Esogetic Colorpuncture, Boulder, Colorado. Her
name is from Osho Rajneesh, the Indian spiritual master with whom she studied
for many years.

Through our observations, it became obvious that long before physical symptoms manifest, bodily changes, disease or illness are energetically present, and through Kirlian photographic technique, reveal themselves.

Peter Mandel, ND
Originator of Esogetic Colorpuncture

Peter Mandel, ND, acupuncturist is well-known in European natural medicine. He has spent the past 20 years researching informative energies and developing related diagnostic systems and therapies. Mandel originated the acu-light therapy system of Esogetic Colorpuncture(TM). He is also the developer of Energy Emission Analysis(TM), a diagnostic system of Kirlian Photography. Mandel is the author of many revolutionary scientific books and articles on new concepts in natural healing techniques including: *Colorpuncture Compendium, Vol.1 and 2; Pharmacy of Light, Vol.1 & 2.* He is the founder of the Mandel Institute for Esogetic Medicine, Germany, and the International Mandel Institute for Esogetic Medicine, Switzerland. The institutes are dedicated to ongoing research and teaching of Mandel's innovative natural healing techniques.

Peter Mandel is the most creative naturopath in the country: he has completely new ideas...that have revolutionized natural healing methods and set them on a modern path.

Joseph Angerer, ND
Founder of the Naturopathic School of Munich
President of the Association of German Naturopaths

Interview With Manohar Croke,
Colorpuncture Therapist

I am at the office of Manohar Croke, Esogetic Colorpuncture therapist. She employs a new European healing technique utilizing colored light, instead of acupuncture needles, to balance the flow of energy in the meridians (pathways of energy in the body). "Using colored light instead of medicine is a gentle, non-invasive way to support all body organs and systems," says Croke.

The peaceful atmosphere in the office is accented by a view of the Rocky Mountains from the window. Croke chose aqua blue for the walls because it is a color that calms the psyche and opens the unconscious.

"Color has certain predictable effects," she tells me, as we sit down and start the interview. "For instance, if you steadily shine blue light on a burn or cut, it will reduce discomfort to the injured area."

BETTE: What do the words "Esogetic" and "Colorpuncture" mean?

MANOHAR: Peter Mandel, the developer of Esogetic Colorpuncture coined the name. Esogetic is a combination of the words "esoteric" and "energetic". Colorpuncture involves the melding of certain esoteric principles of healing with the knowledge of how energy works in the body according to traditional Chinese medicine and modern biophysics.

BETTE: Would you say that acupuncture and light therapy are related to Colorpuncture?

MANOHAR: Yes, but unlike other color therapies, this system applies light to a specific series of acu-points on the skin. Some points are traditional Chinese acupuncture points. Other points are from systems like kinesiology and reflexology. There are also many points and areas on the body authenticated by Mandel.

BETTE: How do you ascertain which points to treat?

MANOHAR: According to the specific physical or psychological healing effect desired.

BETTE: Which colors do you use?

MANOHAR: Light frequencies of red, yellow, blue, green, orange, violet, turquoise, light turquoise, rose, magenta, light green, as well as infrared and three shades of gray light.

BETTE: What do you mean by '"light frequencies"?

MANOHAR: Frequencies of light refers to different wave lengths of electromagnetic vibrations which cause us to see various colors of light. Essentially, the Colorpuncture therapist applies different colors of light to the skin. Each color is precisely set at the midpoint of its wavelength frequency to communicate its own unique inherent energetic information.

BETTE: How does the application of color on acupuncture and other points of the skin cause healing to occur?

MANOHAR: Color stimulates powerful healing impulses which can quickly and powerfully support the body in healing its physical and psychological imbalances. The system was empirically researched by Peter Mandel. It is used systematically to help clients process whatever is held in the unconscious that might be blocking their healing.

BETTE: Does diet, exercise and stress reduction support Colorpuncture treatments?

MANOHAR: It is always good for the body, mind and spirit to eat a healthy diet, exercise and reduce stress. After a Colorpuncture session, we offer clients sound therapy by Mandel for stress reduction. We also instruct clients on how to do home treatment with an acu-light tool on specific points and zones to reduce stress and enhance healing.

BETTE: How difficult would it be for a client to operate the acu-light with some expertise?

MANOHAR: The instruments we send home with the client are set for very precise color frequencies. At the time the tool is made, colors are tested and fall within a very narrow band frequency. This eliminates the need for the client to set the frequencies precisely. Stronger treatments need to be done by a trained Colorpuncture therapist in the clinic office. Through the Esogetic Colorpuncture Institute, we also teach 2-day introductory "self-help" classes, so people can learn several treatments that are useful for maintaining good health and well-being.

BETTE: It sounds like Colorpuncture is compatible with most natural healing approaches.

MANOHAR: It is. Mandel combines Colorpuncture with acupuncture, homeopathy and many other alternative healing methods.

BETTE: How does the body process colored light?

MANOHAR: As light frequencies are absorbed by the skin, they are transmitted along energetic pathway (meridians) which lie deep in the body, stimulating intra-cellular communication which supports life. Light is subtle in its effect, yet fast moving, penetrating deeply into all body cells.

BETTE: Are these facts about light something new that scientists have discovered?

MANOHAR: Certain scientists, like Germany's leading biophysicist Dr. Fritz Albert Popp, now realize that continual electro-magnetic or biophoton light communication between cells is actually the basis for all healthy bodily functions. Biophoton light communication operates at a more fundamental and pervasive level than even the neural messages from the brain, and hormonal messages from the endocrine glands which are generally understood to regulate the body. Peter Mandel has worked in close association with Dr. Popp for many years.

BETTE: What are the attributes of electro-magnetic or biophoton light communication?

MANOHAR: All living cells are constantly emitting a harmonic flow of small particles of light called biophotons. Cells communicate by means of biophotons. Dr. Popp has demonstrated that when cells become diseased, the communication between neighboring cells is disturbed. Peter Mandel's abiding interest has been to develop techniques for restoring balanced biophoton communication between cells, with the strategic application of colored light to the body.

BETTE: How are the colored light frequencies applied to the skin?

MANOHAR: With a hand-held acu-light tool which resembles a small torch or flashlight. It measures about 7 inches in length and a 1/2-inch in diameter. The glass rods inserted in the torch have a tip. They come to a focused unsharpened point, so light can be applied very precisely to one specific acupoint. The tool is manufactured by a German company that works with specifications provided by Peter Mandel.

BETTE: How many Colorpuncture treatments are available?

MANOHAR: There are hundreds of specific Colorpuncture light therapies for a particular sequence of points. Certain prescribed colors are applied to each point in the treatment. The sequence of points and the colors used vary, depending upon what we are trying to effect in the body.

BETTE: Which disorders can Colorpuncture treatments benefit?

MANOHAR: Colorpuncture addresses issues of all sorts concerning health and well-being. For example, there is a Colorpuncture treatment that supports the body in cleaning the lymph system, detoxifying the body and strengthening the immune system. This particular treatment is excellent for any infection, cold, flu, inflammation, or problem with lymph congestion.

BETTE: Is there a light treatment for PMS?

MANOHAR: Yes. I do a light therapy endocrine treatment which helps the hormonal system come into balance to support the body during PMS, menopause and puberty. Endocrine Light Therapy is also useful in cases of shock, trauma, insomnia, stress, anxiety and depression.

BETTE: What colors would you use for endocrine treatment?

MANOHAR: I often use orange and blue, though not exclusively. They are the colors that help balance endocrine function, partly by supporting the pituitary gland. Many Endocrine Therapy treatments will help bring up and release stressor suppressed emotions that tend to distort hormonal functioning.

BETTE: Can you support the body with Colorpuncture in stabilizing and regulating imbalances in different parts of the brain and glandular system ?

MANOHAR: Absolutely. Colorpuncture is beneficial for promoting the synchronization of left and right brain equilibrium. It is also helpful with learning disorders and nervous system disturbances.

BETTE: Do you believe that negative emotion is related to poor health?

MANOHAR: I believe that illness is connected to unresolved emotional conflict from the past or in the present.

BETTE: How do you handle this?

MANOHAR: I use a number of Colorpuncture treatments depending on the client's particular issues, and a Kirlian photograph reading of the client's toe and finger. I often use a Colorpuncture treatment to encourage dreaming. Dreams can bring closure to unprocessed contention by receiving information from our higher self which promotes emotional and physical healing. The dream zone areas on the skin are treated with certain colors, depending upon the "meaning" of a particular zone and its effects.

BETTE: How do you read a Kirlian photo?

MANOHAR: Kirlian readings are very complex. We look for certain energy phenomena such as gaps or excess radiation in certain segments of the fingers and toes which relate to specific areas of the body. This is a technique based on Peter Mandel's years of empirical research on where the meridians run.

BETTE: Would you say that Colorpuncture treatment could motivate us to live out our full potential?

MANOHAR: This is the primary underlying focus of Esogetic Colorpuncture. Peter Mandel believes that in order to heal, a person must come back in contact with their unique potential and truly live it out. Light has a powerful effect on the movement of unconscious material into consciousness. Careful application of light to special points on the skin can help us get in touch with information we need in order to move toward complete healing and expression of ourselves.

BETTE: What Colorpuncture treatment do you use for pain?

MANOHAR: There are many. Since pain is linked to emotional components, we usually include treatments to balance the underlying emotions in conjunction with treatments to relieve the pain. If the emotional cause is not treated and understood, the pain will return, perhaps in a different part of the body.

BETTE: How do you determine where the pain is rooted and what treatment is needed?

MANOHAR: Peter Mandel developed a system called Kirlian Energy Emission Analysis. This entails photographing the light emanating from the client's fingers and toes. Patterns and density of light are studied in detail to accurately assess which Colorpuncture treatment will best restore balance to the energy system. After treatment, another Kirlian photograph provides immediate feedback as to effectiveness of the chosen therapy, and what the next step in the treatment may be.

BETTE: Can you cite cases linking pain to emotional conflicts that were resolved with Colorpuncture therapy?

93

MANOHAR: In one of my clients, I saw signs of old, unresolved emotional conflict that appeared to be the root cause of her intractable symptoms of bronchitis and lung weakness. I administered a Colorpuncture treatment called Conflict Solution therapy. This involved the use of soul-spirit colors: light turquoise, rose, light green and magenta frequencies applied to specific areas of the body in a particular sequence. The procedure helped bring up and release old conflicted emotions which were disturbing her body. She experienced about a week of strong emotions which settled down along with the clearing of her bronchitis condition. Another client complained of pain which showed up in an imprint of a negative parental experience as the possible cause of his discomfort. In Colorpuncture we say, "Sometimes one's mother sits on one's neck." Specific Colorpuncture treatments helped bring up and release the negative imprint of my client's mother on his neck, and his neck pain quickly vanished. At the same time, the client became aware of the way in which he, like his mother, was driven to overwork.

BETTE: On which part of the body is Colorpuncture therapy applied for prenatal trauma?

MANOHAR: Some of these treatments involve points and lines on the feet that relate to every stage of the time spent in the womb, from preconception, conception and on to birth. During treatment the client may actually get in touch with the feelings of wombtime, which, of course, vary from person to person.

BETTE: What feelings could an embryo experience in the womb?

MANOHAR: We underestimated the emotional sensitivity of the baby in the womb. What we know is that the baby is deeply connected to the mother, neurochemically and psychologically. The baby feels all the emotions that the mother is experiencing. A client of mine burst into tears when I treated a point on her foot for the 6th month in the womb. She couldn't figure out her reaction. But later, when she told her mother about this outburst, her mother said that during the 6th month of her pregnancy, she found the clients' father in bed with another woman. The client, as an infant in her mother's womb, retained her mother's traumatic memories of the encounter. For many people, the somatic-emotional memory of traumatic imprints surface into consciousness during or after a Colorpuncture treatment.

BETTE: Do you ever refer clients for psychological care?

MANOHAR: Certainly; if the client wishes me to do so, or if it seems to me that it is in the client's best interests to further exploration of uncovered memories, like sexual abuse, for example. Some of my clients are treated by a psychotherapist at the same time that they are receiving Colorpuncture treatments from me. This creates a powerful synergy of healing. In the absence of psychotherapy, my experience has been that Colorpuncture usually brings up feelings, little by little, like letting steam off a kettle. After a day or two of experiencing old memories and emotions, the treatment is processed through the system. Generally, the client then reports that the upsetting feelings have passed and a relaxed state of well-being has emerged.

BETTE: When a new client comes to your office, do you do a physical exam?

MANOHAR: No, but I take an extensive written history of physical symptoms, health issues, emotional history, current life issues, prenatal history and lifestyle information.

BETTE: Does a client lie down during treatment?

MANOHAR: The client either lies down on a massage treating table or sits up, depending upon which points I am applying light to.

BETTE: Do you play background music during the process?

MANOHAR: I do not generally play music because sound frequencies affect people in various ways. If I use sound in a session, I usually utilize one of Mandel's sound therapies on its own, not as background music. I also talk to the client during treatment to ascertain their reactions to the light, and I do not want the music to distract me or the client.

BETTE: What sensation, if any, is experienced when a color is applied to the skin?

MANOHAR: The client may feel subtle energy or warmth moving in various areas of the body, or a heightened sense of physical and emotional awareness. After treatment, most people feel a sense of relaxation. Depending on the treatment and individual reaction, the client often has vivid dreams resulting in released feelings, new insights, improvement of physical and emotional symptoms and /or a general sense of improved well-being.

BETTE: Can a healing crisis occur after treatment?

MANOHAR: Occasionally a client may develop a mild cold as toxins are discharged from the system. But usually any reaction to Colorpuncture will pass within 3-4 days of treatment and the body will settle into a new balanced alignment.

BETTE: Are your Colorpuncture and Kirlian Energy Emission Analysis workshops offered to laymen?

MANOHAR: Laymen who wish to practice on themselves and their families are welcome, as well as all kinds of health care professionals. We usually teach medical doctors, nurses, psychologists, acupuncturists, naturopaths, body-workers and other healers. We also teach several longer trainings for laymen and professionals interested in becoming professional Colorpuncture practitioners. We always tell them that in order to practice Esogetic Colorpuncture professionally, they need to ascertain the licensing requirements covering the scope of this practice in their State.

BETTE: Why did you become a Colorpuncture therapist?

MANOHAR: I met Peter Mandel in India, at a training he was giving at the Osho Academy of Healing Arts. I was very impressed with the material he was teaching. The treatments I received in that class, as part of the student exchange, along with subsequent treatments from Mr. Mandel and other trained Colorpuncture practitioners, changed my life. Colorpuncture cleared a lot of old fear from my system, freeing me to experience more joy in my life. It brought up and released old buried memories and feelings, in a way that is different from psychotherapy. The experience enabled me to understand myself on a deeper level. Colorpuncpuncture also helped dispel the stress and physical discomforts I was encountering in my body. It enhanced my immune system and strengthened my lungs which were always weak. I was so pleased with my personal experience that I decided to study Esogetic Colorpuncture and utilize it to help other people. About 8 years ago, Peter Mandel asked me to start an Institute in the United States. Since then, together with my co-director, Rosemary Akhila Bourne, I have been privileged to share this magnificent therapy with many healing practitioners around the country.

•••••••••••••••••

*Researchers are becoming convinced that all aspects
of our health are affected by the intensity, duration
and color of the light to which we are exposed.*

Hal Hellman
From: *PSYCHOLOGY TODAY*, April, 1982

•••••••••••••

RECOMENDED READING

*A BIOGRAPHY OF PETER MANDEL,
ORIGINATOR OF ESOGETIC COLORPUNCTURE*
Jack Allanach,
Element Press, 1998

**LIGHT YEARS AHEAD: THE ILLUSTRATED GUIDE TO
FULL SPECTRUM & COLORED LIGHT MIND-BODY HEALING*
Brian Brieling
Celestial Arts Publishing, 1996

**NOTE: This book includes an article by Manohar Croke
describing her work with Esogetic Colorpuncture.*

•••••••••••••••••

For information about treatments with
Manohar Croke, or programs offered at the
Institute for Esogetic Colorpuncture, contact:

Institute For Esogetic Colorpuncture
1705 14th Street #198
Boulder, CO 80302
Phone: (303) 443-1666
website: www.colorpuncture.com
email: abhmanohar@aol.com

For information on treatments
or training in California contact:

Institute for Esogetic Colorpuncture
PO Box 3013
San Anselmo, CA 94979
Phone: (415) 461-6641
email: rosemary@colorpuncture.com

•••••••••••••••••

9

REMOTE SPIRIT DEPOSSESSION
Barbara Duncan and Jack Keck

....

..the body is a supersensitive individual entity who has allowed itself through study, through opening the (gland) centers of the body, to become possessed with reflexes and activities outside of itself...

Q-3. *How did I happen to pick this up?*
A-3. *...the body in its study opened the (gland) centers and allowed self to become sensitive to outside influences.*
Q-4. *What is it exactly that assails me?*
A-4. *Outside influences. Discarnate entities.*

EDGAR CAYCE
Reading 5221-1

―――――――――

Barbara Duncan, MA, Cht, RHA, and a Ph.D. candidate at St. Johns University, Springfield, LA., is a certified clinical Hypnotherapist on the National Board for Hypnotherapy and Hypnotic Anesthesiology. She is a member of the National Guild of Hypnotists, and the National Society of Clinical Hypnotherapists who voted her "Member of the Year", in 1993. Duncan studied remote depossession with Dr. Irene Hickman, author of *Remote Depossession,* and subsequently added spirit releasement techniques to her long list of credits. Duncan is the only hypnotist accepted into the Medical, Psychological and Legal Society (MPALS) of Houston, Texas.

Jack Keck is a Certified Clinical Hypnotherapist with the National Board for Hypnotherapy and Hypnotic Anesthesiology. He is also a Registered Professional Engineer.

99

LECTURE ON REMOTE SPIRIT DEPOSSESSION
Presented By: Barbara Duncan and Jack Keck

I felt anxious about attending the lecture on Remote Spirit Depossession. Barbara Duncan and Jack Keck were presenting it at the University of Houston, Houston, Texas, on behalf of the A.R.E. Holistic Exposition. I had been terrified when I saw the movie *The Exorcist* and wondered if the facts conveyed at the Duncan/Keck lecture would horrify me, too. However, curiosity won out over my apprehension. I found myself in a large audience listening to the very credible lecture about the Duncan/Keck team and their extraordinary career in Remote Spirit Depossession. Duncan, a mild-mannered, polite, middle-aged woman was dressed in a business suit. She looked more like a college professor than someone involved in dealing with spirit attachments. Duncan explained to the audience that she worked as a team with Hypnotherapist Jack Keck in conducting remote spirit releasement sessions because the process required two people. Duncan/Keck scan the applicant to determine whether there are entities or attachments on and/or in the person's body.

The process begins when a person submits an application with information about the individual who may be having the session. A reason for the session does not have to be given. But if it is included, Duncan/Keck do not read it until the final scanning is completed. This insures that the information in no way influences the session. The application should include a specific time, date and location where the person could be found within the past 30 days. Duncan/Keck have discovered that this data assists them in projecting their minds to "locate" the person at the beginning of the session. The process is always done remotely so that it is possible to help people anywhere.

Duncan explained to the audience that communication via the five senses on the three-dimensional earth plane is what everyone is familiar with - third level vibration. When a session is begun, the communication senses shift from the third level vibration to the fifth level vibration. "Seeing" and "hearing" is done in the mind. The same vibrational shift takes place when we go into meditation. This is how the higher self of one person can communicate with the higher self of another person. It is also known as ESP.

The person to be scanned does not have to be in the presence of Duncan/Keck. For example, a mother or father can request a session for their young child, a grandparent for a grandchild, a husband for his wife and vice versa. The conscious self of the person on the application does not have to be informed about the request being made in his/her behalf, because before the session begins, permission must be obtained from the higher self of that person.

Duncan/Keck's higher selves communicate on a spiritual level, with the higher self of the person to be scanned, to request permission to do the session. If the higher self of the person to be scanned refuses after Duncan/Keck make the request on three different occasions, the application is returned. Although refusal from the higher self is rare, it has occurred. If the answer is yes, then Duncan/Keck, in an altered state, scan the body for attachments. Working in the fifth dimension vibrations, the person is "seen" and slowly rotated in space so all areas of the body can be scanned. Duncan makes notes as Keck does the initial scanning and when this is completed, she does a follow-up scanning, in the altered state, so that they have two different perspectives.

The aura, Duncan explained, is a protective energy shield around all living bodies. A diminished aura, which is like having a weakened immune system, is a condition that makes it easy for a spirit to inhabit a body. This may occur when a person experiences, for example, inordinately strong emotions such as extreme anger, jealousy, hate, greed, excessive physical exertion and even a powerfully sudden jolt in an automobile collision. The use of alcohol and drugs, and even a severe illness, can also lower the aura energy. But the more spiritual a person is, the stronger the aura.

Duncan/Keck begin the session by scanning the person externally. External attachments take a variety of forms. "Sometimes they are contoured like an octopus with long tentacles, or a blob of color, or some even take the form of a crustacean," Duncan explained. Often, she finds the crustacean-type of entity in people with very bad sinus problems. One of her clients did not mention his sinus problems when he requested a remote session. During the session, Duncan/Keck found a large crustacean-shaped attachment over the man's sinus cavity. They removed the attachment, and when the man wrote to them four months later, he said that he had been meaning to write sooner about his sinus problem disappearing, but he wanted to make certain it was permanent. He told them that he had suffered with chronic sinus problems for five years, but they immediately disappeared after his remote session. Four years later he wrote again to advise Duncan/Keck that he was still free of sinus problems.

Duncan said that, generally, external attachments are not here to deliberately cause harm. However, they drain energy while they are attached, not to mention the emotions such as fear and anxiety that may be generated when the person is aware, on some level, of the attachments presence. Duncan/Keck request angelic assistance to accomplish permanently returning external attachments to their own time and dimension. All areas that were previously occupied with external attachments are filled with healing Light energy.

In another example of an external attachment, a mother requested a session for her eight-month-old child. She explained that from the time her baby came into the world, he would sleep for short periods of time, then awaken screaming. This was a repetitive pattern throughout the day and night. Also, with the exception of his father, he had an abnormal fear of men. During the session for the child, Duncan/Keck found an external attachment which looked like the head of a shrimp located directly in front of his face. The child woke up screaming because he was frightened. When he closed his eyes, he "saw" the shrimp-like attachment in his mind. First, Duncan/Keck removed the attachment and then they "asked" the child's higher self why he feared men. They were informed by the child's higher self that in a past lifetime he was a female of great power who had abused many men. In the next lifetime, once again, he was a female, but in different circumstances. As a female, he was gang raped by a group of old-world sailors. The first past lifetime set up the personal retribution that took place in the second lifetime. This accounted for the extreme fear of men that was retained from that lifetime into the present one. The higher selves of Duncan/Keck communicated these facts with the child's higher self. After the session, the mother reported that the child slept peacefully that night without awakening. Shortly afterward, she reported that the child's fear of men had disappeared and that he was continuing to sleep peacefully.

There are many ways external attachments can affect people. "We had a session with a woman who had a large attachment on the back of her head that had taken the form of a giant sea slug," Duncan said. "It had been with the woman since she was a child, and as she grew, it also grew." When they scanned the woman, they "saw" that the attachment had extended itself around both sides of her face, partially covering both of her eyes like blinders on a horse. After Duncan/Keck removed the attachment, the woman said that she finally felt she was no longer being surrounded by some kind of pressure around her head.

Attachments are not the only things that can affect someone externally. Duncan said that there have been a few occasions when her higher self revealed that strong negative energy, taking the form of a curse, had been projected onto someone. These cases take several days and require a special procedure that neutralizes the effect of the curse. Sometimes the curse has been with the person for a number of lifetimes. All past lifetimes influenced by this curse must be removed so that the curse does not come forward to affect a future lifetime.

For example, the father of a teenage girl requested a session for her because he felt that she was not acting like a typical teenager. He intuitively felt something was very wrong beyond the ordinary. In addition, his daughter was very fragile and unstable. Upon initiating the session, the higher selves of Duncan/Keck were advised by the girl's higher self that a curse had been placed on her in a past lifetime, when she had been a male living in England in the 1850s. He had traveled to Central Africa where he had gotten into a conflict with the local natives. In retaliation, they placed a curse on him - one that remained with him into the present lifetime as a young girl. Duncan/Keck removed the curse, and subsequently the father advised them that the girl had totally changed. He also stated that he had been aware, before he received Duncan/Keck's report, of the time that the session had been completed due to the change in her personality.

Once all external attachments have been cleared, Duncan/Keck begin scanning for internal attachments. The first one is an earthbound spirit that left its body at the time of its death, but remains on the earth plane instead of going into Light to learn, grow and progress. There are many reasons, according to Duncan, why this phenomenon occurs. Sometimes an earthbound spirit has had a very traumatic death. She cited a client who had a spirit attached to him that had died in a fire. "The spirit was fearful of going into the Light because of his association with the brightness of the fire which had caused his death. So, he had attached himself to my client for refuge," Duncan explained. She warned the audience that hospitals, funeral homes, hospice nursing homes and cemeteries are places where a lot of spirits can be found looking for a place to go.

In some cases, the attachment may be a spirit that is so connected to things on earth, like members of its family, a spouse, a mother, a child, property it owned or a house that it lived in when it was alive, that it does not want to leave the earth. Instead, it stays around the things it cared about and often attaches itself to a loved one. "Many times spirits attach themselves to people who remind them of somebody dear to them," Duncan said. "I persuaded the spirit of a mother to leave and go into the Light when I found her attached to a young woman who reminded her of her daughter whom she missed very much."

There is also a category of spirits known as "walk-in's", another group of earth bound spirits. Duncan spoke of a lady who came to her and Keck requesting a session for her husband who had serious and unusual problems. Upon scanning him internally, Duncan/Keck determined that an alien had taken over his body and was controlling it. Duncan/Keck removed the alien and the wife was advised to watch her husband for the next three days and report his status. A three-day period of seventy-two hours has been found to be the normal time for a change to become evident. The wife reported that during the first two days, her husband spent the majority of his day seated in a chair slumped forward with his chin on his chest. On the third day, he began to move around and talk to her for the first time since the alien removal had taken place. By the end of the third day, he was up and moving about normally, but his personality had changed completely. He had become spiritual whereas before, he had ridiculed his wife for her spirituality. In addition to now loving the arts and literature, the husband was completely different in composure, speech and personality. His wife said that he was the soul mate she had always wanted. In a follow-up session, the higher selves of Duncan/Keck confirmed that a "walk-in" had entered the husbands body upon the alien's departure.

Revenge can be another factor involved in spirit attachment. Some people may have had a severe problem with someone during their lifetime. When they die, if their spirit seeks revenge, they may choose to attach to the person with whom they had the problem and do everything they can to confuse, disorient or alter the personality of the one they hated. "Some earthbound spirits may believe they will go to hell when they die and prefer staying on earth where they think they will be safe," Duncan told the audience. "And other earthbound spirits may have a lot of shame because of something they have done in their life and do not feel worthy of going to the Light." She recalled a session where the spirit of a son refused to go to the Light because he had lead a bad life, and he did not feel worthy of being anywhere his deceased mother was.

Many earthbound spirits attach themselves to a loving person because they want to help that individual. Duncan talked about a spirit depossession of a mother who attached herself to her son. The son was 68 years old and the mother was still telling him what to do. When he died and his father's spirit came to take him into the Light, she was still telling the spirit of her son what to do. "In some cases children have asked their parents to stay with them, because they need their warmth and protection," Duncan explained. "But this is not good for the child who needs to become independent, nor is it good for the spirit of the parent who must go to the Light where it can grow, advance and perhaps reincarnate into another body."

Part of the process for removing earthbound spirits is getting members of the family and/or friends, or anyone who cares and loves the earthbound spirit, to come out of the Light, become visible and communicate with the earthbound. This is comforting to the earthbound soul. Typically, the earthbound soul is assisted by angels from this side to the edge of the Light where family members are waiting. Then they all walk into the Light together and disappear.

In one of Duncan's clients she found the earthbound spirit of an American Indian Viet Nam Veteran. When he died, his spirit was looking for a vehicle to take him to New Mexico, his homeland. The soldier next to him, who was Duncan's client, was from Texas. The spirit decided to get into the body of the Texan expecting to leave the body after the soldier returned to Texas, and then go back to his home in New Mexico. "But the Indian spirit's plan didn't work,"

Duncan stated. "Instead, it was trapped in the Texan's body for many years until he was released during the session." When family members were asked to come from the Light for this Indian spirit, the deceased members of the tribe came out of the Light for him, and there was a marvelous reunion."

She also told the audience that some people who were addicted to food, tobacco, alcohol and/or drugs when they were alive, reject going to the Light when they die, in favor of attaching themselves to a living person with the same addiction. They want to continue the familiar feelings of their substance abuse. Duncan said that she has even encountered spirits who starved to death during their lifetime. Instead of going to the Light, they attached themselves to the body of a person who was overweight. "These obese people cannot lose weight while the attachment is in them. Every time an attempt would be made to do so, something would sabotage the effort and result in an overwhelming eating compulsion," Duncan explained. "That "something" is the earthbound spirit attachment who starved to death and never wanted to be hungry again."

There are some people who may have an inherent weakness for attracting spirits. Duncan said this could be due to their subconscious allowing particular spirits to come into them as a karmic or contractual pay back. "There are even cases where a spirit has followed another spirit into a body," she told listeners. Two sisters had attached to one of her clients. When the younger sister died, her spirit joined itself to the client's body. Upon the death of the older sister, her spirit followed the younger sister's spirit into the body of the client. "The older sister still wanted to control her younger sister as she had done throughout their lifetime."

The second category of attachment is the dark entity, sometimes called a demon. These attachments are harmful and may cause degeneration in the body. Sometimes they may even be the primary cause of the death of the person. People who believe they hear voices may often be possessed by dark entities. "I had a client who had several operations that she could not heal from," Duncan said. "When I did a session with her, I found a large dark entity in the area of the abdomen where the surgery had been performed." After Duncan/Keck removed the dark entity, the woman began healing normally.

In the case of a dark entity, Duncan/Keck persuade it to change into a light being and leave the body permanently. They work to remove any type of spirit attachment on a lasting basis so it never joins anyone again. If they have difficulty with permanent removal and conversion of a dark entity into a light being, Duncan/Keck call upon the forces of St. Michael whom they believe are always there to help. All life and energy forms originally came from God. Many have grown so distant from God that they can not even remember His existence.

Once they are shown the spark of light that exists in all beings, and persuaded that they can change, they do so. This is the option of "free will" that all life forms are given by God. "Some of the forces of St. Michael were formerly dark entities who converted into light workers," Duncan stated. "Once a dark entity is convinced to become a light worker, we ask the dark entity to look inside itself where there is always a spark of light." When the dark entity acknowledges the light within itself, the light begins to grow until the dark entity is filled with its own light. It then has no problem leaving the body it had invaded to go to the Light.

The third category of attachments is alien implants, which are not spirits, but actual mechanical-type devices that come in all shapes and sizes. Duncan has found them in different parts of the human body. She believes they are there to gather data. The implants are placed in the human body to collect information about the human culture and transmit it back to the alien's home base. The reason these devices cannot normally be seen is that they are made of fifth level vibrations. "Humans are different from all other life forms due to their capabilities for love and compassion," Duncan said. "Thus, humans are an anomaly to other advanced life forms in the universe who constantly collect data on us."

Duncan cited a session in which she and Keck found an alien implant in an applicant. It was shaped like a mask covering the man's entire head. "Sometimes alien implants are little probes, but this one was the largest alien implant we had ever seen," she explained. The gentleman complained of chronic pain for 33 years and said that he had tried every possible treatment to rid himself of discomfort, but nothing had worked. After Duncan/Keck removed the alien implant, they discovered that the man, a Vietnam Veteran, also had earthbound attachments.

According to Duncan, it is not unusual to find earthbound attachments in the Vietnam Veterans who request sessions. Many spirit attachments were soldiers in Vietnam who met with tragic circumstances, losing their lives in battle. Some were blown away by enemy fire without even a body left for identification. When this happened, it was as though their spirits were suddenly and violently separated from their bodies. Often, these spirits will not acknowledge that they are dead. Typically, they will join the first live person that is near them, usually another Vietnam soldier on the battlefield, in order to resume the sensation of life. Some attach to another soldier because they do not want to be left in a foreign country, but want to return home.

Duncan/Keck removed all of the attachments from their Vietnam Veteran client. The next day, he told them that he was very tired and had to rest, but he was totally pain free for the first time in many years. In the following days, his energy level steadily rose and soon he was able to do a full day's work. Three years later he reported that he was still pain free and functioning optimally. His physician called Duncan to ask why the gentleman had changed so much. "I have been working with this man for over 20 years, and he was always belligerent, rude and offensive. Now he's courteous, refined, loving, has a good attitude and a body that is completely changed for the better," the medical doctor said.

In another session with a woman who was complaining about personality changes in herself, Duncan/Keck found that she was attached by an alien who had slowly come through her back and mimicked whatever she did. It was like two people walking in unison, one in back of the other. For a long time she was unaware of anything wrong, but as the alien began exerting the influence of its own personality over her, people began to make remarks about the changes in her personality. "Once we removed it, she was able to reclaim her normal personality," said Duncan.

Someone in the audience wanted to know how one could protect themselves from spirit attachments entering the body. Duncan's answer was to fill yourself with the universal white Christ Light first thing each morning. Begin by shutting your eyes and visualizing the white Light coming in through the top of your head and completely filling your entire body with the white Light. Next, extend the white Light outward, as though the white Light is coming out of every pore of your body, until you are inside a large bubble of white Light. Do the same thing in the evening before you go to bed. Anytime you think about protection from spirit attachments, call upon the white Christ Light to fill you. She also said that prayer is very effective for warding off spirit attachments, and that some people, through their own spiritual beliefs and perseverance can reject attached spirits. "But, this may take a long time and repeated attempts, especially if the spirit attachment is stubborn and rejects the person's efforts," Duncan pointed out. "For most untrained people, it is not a good idea to tackle the spirit world."

She reminded the audience that Edgar Cayce cautioned against using channeling devices like the ouija board, because it is possible to pick up dark spirits and other negative entities by doing so. This is due to the fact that you may set up the intent in your mind to make the connection with any entity that comes, and you lack the experience to appropriately protect yourself before proceeding. All spirits that come with information are not necessarily good spirits, and sometimes you get a lot more then you planned for.

"One of my clients read a book on channeling and decided to give it try. She had done some past life regression work when she was a young girl, and she wanted to communicate with an old lover from a past lifetime," Duncan told the audience. "She discovered her natural ability to channel. The first time she tried it, she opened the door to the "other side". Her client told Duncan that soon afterwards, she felt the same warm, loving feelings she once shared with her lover, and even heard their familiar music being played. But one night when she went to bed, she felt hands massaging her feet. She thought it was her lover until she experienced the feeling of something probing in her brain to the point of pain. When she turned the light on, it all disappeared. Terrified, she called a psychic who assisted in "closing" the door to the spirit world. Unfortunately, the door did not remain closed, and before long the same experiences happened once again. She contacted Duncan/Keck for help. The remote session was begun with Duncan/Keck asking their higher selves for assistance. They called upon anyone who could help them to come, with the stipulation that this help must be willing to stand in the Light with them. "In cases where we have no experience, we will use this procedure to call on assistance from the "other side". As long as anyone who comes can stand in the white Light, the help is accepted." Duncan advised that before any help is accepted, it should always be challenged by placing it in the white Light because things may not be what they seem. Even angelic-looking beings may be wolves in sheep's clothing. An old American Indian Shaman, who passed the Light test, came to join them in solving the problem. With the use of smudging, dancing, chanting and other rituals, he succeeded in permanently closing the door to the spirit world. As soon as the session was completed, the client telephoned Duncan to say that she "knew" the instant the door was closed, and that she would never open it again.

Before I left the lecture, I picked up an application from Duncan and Keck, just in case I ever needed their services. And I made a mental note to fill myself with Christ light, and pray for myself and loved ones to divert spirit attachments that may be eyeing us up as hosts. Spooky - but not as terrifying as the movie "The *Exorcist*", knowing that Duncan/Keck are there to help.

Contact Barbara Duncan and Jack Keck at:

Phone: (713) 774 - 1877
email: j.keck@wt.net

––––––––––––––––––––

RECOMMENDED READING

SPIRIT RELEASEMENT THERAPY GAINING ACCEPTANCE
J. Chambers
Venture Inward Sept/Oct, pp. 17-18, A.R.E. Press, 1994

REMOTE DEPOSSESSION
I. Hickman
Hickman Systems, 1994

SPIRIT RELEASEMENT THERAPY
W. Baldwin,
The Human Potential Foundation Press, 1991

THE UNQUIET DEAD
E. Fiore
Ballantine Publishing Group, 1997

10

COOKING THE AYURVEDIC WAY
A Class With David Broussard

....

Be mindful of the diet that it is kept proper. Take time to eat and to eat the right thing. Then give time for the digestive forces to act before becoming so mentally and bodily active as to upset the digestion.

EDGAR CAYCE
Reading 243-P-17

....

David Broussard is the Director at the Ayurvedic Center, Houston, Texas. He graduated from Washington and Lee University, earning a Master's Degree in Wellness Sciences. Broussard also attended the Ayurvedic Institute, Albuquerque, New Mexico, studying under the direction of Dr. Vasant Lad. He is a certified practitioner of Ayurvedic Lifestyle Management, and a Postural Integration Bodywork and Polarity Therapist. Broussard also trained in the Dialogue Process at the Option Institute and Fellowship, Sheffield, Massachusetts.

....

...The emphasis on local and seasonal foods is not unique to the Cayce diet. The ancient traditional healing systems of Chinese and (Indian) Ayurvedic medicine teach that, in order to maintain health, we must live in harmony with nature and balance our body energies according to seasons and local climate. To a large extent this is accomplished through foods and herbs with certain seasonal qualities.

Simone Gabbay, Nutritional Consultant
From: *VENTURE INWARD, "Locally-Grown and Seasonal Foods"*
March/April 1996

110

I am at an Ayurvedic cooking class at the Ayurvedic Center, Houston, Texas. Director David Broussard, a relaxed, soft spoken, middle-aged man, greets us. "Tonight you will learn to prepare light, nourishing meals using the principles of Ayurveda to stay healthy throughout the seasons." He explains that "Ayur" means health or life, and "Veda" means knowledge or science. Ayurveda, the "Science of Health" is from India. For over six-thousand years it has proven its effectiveness in promoting healthy lifestyles, optimum health and longevity. According to Ayurveda, individuality results from a unique combination of three basic operating principles in nature: Vata, Pitta and Kapha - Sanskrit words. Understanding our individuality gives us a direction for creating health and happiness.

Vata governs motion in the body, breathing, circulation, elimination and the flow of nerve impulses to and from the brain. People with balanced Vata constitutions are, by nature, cold, dry, mobile, alert, creative and enthusiastic. When Vata types are out of balance they can be prone to worry and distraction.

Pitta governs digestion, metabolism and processing of food, air and water throughout the body. Pitta types are hot and precise by nature. In balance, Pitta's have good digestion, sharp intellect and are warm and confident. Out of balance, Pitta's anger easily, are overly intense and bothered by heat.

Kapha governs structure and the forming of muscle, fat, bone and sinew. Kapha types have solid builds, are calm, stable, affectionate and steady by nature when balanced. Lethargy, possessiveness and overweight are out of balance characteristics for Kapha types.

"Everyone has certain Vata, Pitta and Kapha qualities," Mr. Broussard explains. "Ayurveda looks for predominant constitutional qualities to determine your needs for health, happiness, dietary requirements and exercise."

He tells us that vivacious Vata types benefit from simple, nourishing food and regular routine. They tend to be cool natured and dry out, so they need a warm moistening diet for balance. Since Pitta people have a lot of heat in them, they need a cooling, drying diet and leisure time for enjoyment to offset their intense schedules. Solid Kapha's require a spicier diet and stimulating activities. They tend to be bigger people who have a problem with excess mucus. For Kapha's, warm, dry foods are balancing. A condition that remains out of balance will eventually produce what conventional medicine calls disease. "Our system must be in balance to use its energy for extracting the life force from elements that give us good health and vitality," Mr. Broussard tells us.

We are invited into his kitchen. He hands out a quiz to determine what our Ayurvedic constitutional type would be. I answer the questions and discover that

I am a combination of Vata and Pitta, with more Pitta qualities. (*See questionnaire at the end of this chapter to determine your Ayurveic body type.*)

Ayurveda says that each season goes with a constitutional type and impacts us by its attributes: warm, dry, cool, damp. Mr. Broussard tells us that we are going to have a cooling, summery dinner because it is hot and damp in Houston. "Food can keep our constitutions balanced throughout the seasons," he says. And he explains that if you moved from Houston to a dry climate, no matter what your constitutional type is, foods that moisten would keep you from drying out and supply you with more energy.

"The menu tonight includes classic staples: mung beans, boiled basmati rice, steamed in-season vegetables, raisin chutney and rice khir for dessert," he announces.

I discover that mung beans are little, nutty flavored beans. They resemble split peas and are shelled and skinned, which makes them cook faster. Mr. Broussard is going to make an Indian dish called Yellow Mung Dal. Dal means bean soup. He will puree the beans by whisking them after they are cooked, and use them as a topping over the rice. He rinses the beans 5 times before soaking them in 4 cups of water. Then he adds a few drops of olive oil and turmeric. The mixture is brought to a boil on a medium heat, which is then lowered. The beans simmer for 20 minutes as the rice boils.

"This is long-grain rice, precooked before it was hulled, so all the nutrients were driven back into it. Long-grain rice is easier to digest than brown rice and has a cooling energy to it," he tells us. The rice is slightly dirty, so he rinses it until the water runs clear. Then he places the rice in a glass pot with a half-inch of cold water, covers it and brings it to a boil on a medium heat. The heat is decreased to a low flame and the rice cooks for 20 minutes until it absorbs the water.

"The vegetables of the day are locally grown broccoli and carrots," Mr. Broussard tells the class. Instead of a leafy vegetable, like a salad, which has a cooling, lighter energy, he has chosen vegetables that are a little heavier because they are more nourishing. He places the vegetables in a glass pot with a half-inch of water and steams them. "We'll also have raisin chutney which is easy to make, and most people like it."

Chutney has a warming energy, supports good digestion and helps bring out the flavor in other foods. It has all 6 tastes that the body requires to feel satisfied: sweet, sour, salty, bitter, astringent and pungent. He places 1 cup of raisins, half-a-teaspoon of cayenne, 4 tablespoons of water, 1 tablespoon of fresh ginger, half-a-teaspoon of salt and half-a-lime into a blender. The ingredients are blended into a coarse paste, poured into a Pyrex dish, and placed into the refrigerator.

"For dessert we will have rice khir," Mr. Broussard says, as he begins to soak a pinch of saffron in 1 tablespoon of milk for 10 minutes. Indian puddings, or khirs, are often spiced with saffron and cardamom, not only because these spices are tasty, but also because they help counteract the mucus-forming effects of milk. He heats a medium-sized pot and adds half-a-cup of ghee - clarified butter with no oxidized cholesterol or hydrogenated fat in it. A half-cup of creamed rice is stirred in, until the mixture is light brown and fragrant. It is followed by 8 cups of milk, the soaked saffron, 1 heaping tablespoon of sliced almonds, 1 cup of Sucanat, and one-quarter teaspoon of cardamom. "You can also use another type of sugar besides Sucanat for this recipe," he says. "In India, granulated Jaggary would be used."

He explains that Jaggary is a natural unprocessed sugar from sugar cane juice. "When Jaggary is not available," he says, "Turbinado and Sucanat are good natural sugar cane juice substitutes." To prevent lumps from forming, he stirs the mixture for a few minutes as it is brought to a boil. "Kapha's should eat this dessert only occasionally," he tells us as he turns off the heat and covers the pot. In Ayurvedic tradition, desserts usually are served with the main meal, because eating sweets at the end of the meal could cause congestion and sinus problems.

A woman in the class asks, "What can I do to make my kids healthier? They are overweight and have chronic mucus and colds." Mr. Broussard tells her that too many sweets clog up the body and cause weight gain. Bitter foods help cleanse the system, but our culture over-emphasizes sweet tastes and under-emphasizes bitter tastes. Vegetables are often pungent or bitter-sweet, so most American children do not like them. Many traditions have bitter herbs and slightly bitter teas. Japanese restaurants, for example, serve slightly bitter green teas, because the Japanese culture cultivates bitter tastes that help cleanse the body. "The answer to better health in children and adults is to balance one's tastes," Mr. Broussard tells us. "A balanced body supports good digestion and assimilation of nutrients and minerals."

He shows the class his spice container - a round stainless steel bowl containing 6 jars of turmeric, cumin seed, salt, mustard, fennel and celery seed. I learn that, like human beings, foods and spices have characteristics: cool/dry, cool/damp, warm/dry, warm/damp. We can balance our properties and needs by choosing the right foods and spices. There are warming and drying foods like ginger, tea and cayenne, or spicier foods that break up mucus and keep things moving in the system. "The turmeric I added to the mung beans is dry, pungent and bitter. It's a natural antibiotic. Tumeric is good for ridding the body of excess mucus and congestion."

He shows us a chart with guidelines for a healthy constitutional balance:

TASTE	ENERGY	EFFECT
Sweet	Cooling	Moistens
Sour	Heating	Moistens
Salty	Heating	Moistens
Bitter	Cooling	Drying
Astringent	Drying	Cooling
Pungent	Heating	Drying

The sweet category, I learn, does not mean sugar, pastry or candy; instead it means grains, meats, sweet fruits and vegetables. "There are exceptions to these guidelines," Mr. Broussard says. "Honey, for example, is sweet and has a heating/drying energy." Other exceptions are lemons, which are sour and have a cooling/moistening effect, and ginger, which is pungent and has a heating/moistening effect. "When a Vata person gets a Kapha imbalance, like a cold, eating drying energy Kapha foods that are bitter, astringent and pungent, will help the body dry out the cold and balance itself," he says.

As Mr. Broussard whisks the mung beans, he explains that these beans are a very digestible form of high quality protein. They are even more digestible than soy products which have a lot of enzyme inhibitors in them. He heats 2 tablespoons of olive oil in a pan. It spatters as he adds one-and-a-half- teaspoons of cumin seed. The oil and cumin seed are poured over the dal, followed by one-half-cup of chopped tomato, one-quarter-cup of chopped onion, one-quarter-cup of chopped cilantro, and pepper and salt. The ingredients are covered and simmered for 15 minutes. "It smells so good," I tell Mr. Broussard.

He asks the class to get plates. We line up and Mr. Broussard serves us buffet style: yellow mung dal over boiled basmati rice, steamed vegetables, chutney on the side and rice khir for dessert. "The colors of the food are pretty," a student remarks. We sit at the kitchen table and start eating the meal.

"Please help yourself to some water," Mr. Broussard points to a pitcher. "Water can be a cool temperature, but never icy cold. Ice is a shock to the system and suppresses digestion."

"Is our dinner for all constitutional types?" someone asks.

"You can balance out foods to meet your constitutional requirements," Mr. Broussard explains. "Broccoli, for example, has a pungent, astringent energy. However, if you add a little olive oil on the broccoli it becomes more balanced for a Vata type."

The food is tasty and I enjoy eating it. While we are having our dinner, Mr. Broussard discusses food combinations to avoid. "Milk is incompatible with banana, meat, fish, melons, curd, sour fruits, kichari, bread containing yeast and cherries." He tells us that poor food combinations result in indigestion and gas, which interferes with our Vata, Pitta and Kapha state. The disturbance can cause a toxic condition responsible for many ailments. (*See "Food Combinations To Avoid" at the end of this chapter*).

"My diet, up until now, has not been a healthy one," a woman in the class confides. "How can I detoxify my body?" Mr. Broussard suggests herbal supplements to reduce toxins in the body, and encourage good digestion and assimilation. Other measures are fasting according to body type, reducing water when appropriate, indulging in light exercise and getting plenty of sunshine and fresh air. He explains that toxins are a byproduct of incomplete digestion. They consist of raw, undigested and nonhomogenous substances in the body that block cellular respiration. This creates a heavy lethargic feeling, weakening of the immune system and eventually the cause of disease. Signs of body toxins are: weakness, desire for stimulants, foul breath, flatulence, coating on the tongue, body odor and lack of inspiration. Some causes of toxicity are: overeating, eating when not hungry, eating before digestion of the previous meal, poor food combinations, refined and processed foods, wrong foods for the season, iced drinks with meals and incomplete chewing.

It has been a very informative evening with an introduction to many delicious flavors and aromas. "I had no idea that healthy, balanced Ayurvedic foods would be such a tasty experience!" I tell Mr. Broussard.

••••••••••••••••

Contact Mr. David Broussard at:

The Ayurvedic Center
4100 Westheimer, Suite 235
Houston, Texas 77027
Telephone or Fax: 713-436-2525
Website: www.holhealth.com

DISCOVER YOUR AYURVEDIC CONSTITUTION

Guidelines For Taking The Test:

Read each question and make a check if you feel it describes you. Answer questions according to how they apply over time, rather then just recent history. When you have completed all three sections, add the check marks in each section to produce your scores for Vata, Pitta and Kapha.

Your highest score is the principle that is predominant in your mind and body. For example, if Vata is the highest score, then you are a Vata type. However, if two columns have similar scores, then a combination of two principles dominates in your constitution. For example, you may be a Vata-Pitta or Pitta-Kapha.

VATA is cold, dry and moving by nature:

0   You perform activity very quickly.
0   You are good at memorizing recent things and then not remembering
    them later.
0   You are enthusiastic and vivacious by nature.
0   You have a thin physique and do not gain weight easily.
0   You have always learned new things very quickly.
0   Your characteristic gait while walking is light and quick.
0   You tend to have difficulty making decisions.
0   You tend to develop gas or become constipated easily.
0   You tend to have cold hands and feet.
0   You become anxious or worried frequently.
0   You can not tolerate cold weather as well as most people.
0   You speak quickly and friends think that you are talkative.
0   Your moods change easily, and you are somewhat emotional by nature.
0   You often have difficulty in falling asleep or having a sound night's sleep.
0   Your skin tends to be very dry, especially in the winter.
0   Your mind is very active, sometimes restless, but also very imaginative.
0   Your movements are quick and active; your energy tends to come in bursts.

PITTA is hot and precise by nature:

0   You consider yourself to be very efficient.

0   In your activities you tend to be extremely precise and orderly.

0   You are strong-minded and have a somewhat forceful manner.

0   You feel uncomfortable or easily fatigued in hot weather.

0   You tend to perspire easily.

0   Even though you might not always show it, you become irritable or angry quite easily.

0   If you skip a meal or a meal is delayed, you become uncomfortable.

0   One or more of the following characteristics describes your hair: early graying or balding, thin, fine, straight hair, blonde, reddish or sandy-colored hair.

0   You have a strong appetite.

0   Many people consider you stubborn.

0   You are very regular in your bowel habits - it would be more common for you to have loose stools than to be constipated.

0   You become impatient very easily.

0   You tend to be a perfectionist about details.

0   You get angry quite easily but then quickly forget about it.

0   You are very fond of cold foods, ice cream and ice-cold drinks.

0   You are more likely to feel that a room is too hot than too cold.

0   You don't tolerate foods that are very hot and spicy.

KAPHA is steady and solid by nature:

0   Your natural tendency is a to do things in a slow and relaxed fashion.

0   You gain weight more easily than most people and lose it more slowly.

0   You have a placid and calm disposition; you are not easily ruffled.

0   You can skip meals easily without any significant discomfort.

0   You have a tendency toward excess mucus, phlegm, chronic congestion, asthma or sinus problems.

0   You must have at least eight hours of sleep in order to be comfortable the next day.

0   You sleep very deeply.

0   You are very calm by nature and not easily angered.

0   You do not learn as quickly as some people, but you have excellent retention and a long memory.

117

0   You have a tendency toward becoming plump.

0   Weather that is cool and damp bothers you.

0   Your hair is thick, dark and wavy.

0   You have smooth, soft skin.

0   You have a large, solid body build.

0   The following words describe you well: serene, sweet-natured, affectionate and forgiving.

0   You have slow digestion, which makes you feel heavy after eating.

0   You have very good stamina, physical endurance and a steady level of energy.

0   You generally walk with a slow, measured gait.

....

FOOD COMBINATIONS TO AVOID

Milk is incompatible with: banana, meat, fish, melons, curd, sour fruits, kichari, bread containing yeast and cherries.

Melons are incompatible with: grains, starch, fried foods and cheese.

Starches are incompatible with: eggs, chai, milk, banana, dates and persimmon.

Honey is incompatible with ghee, in equal proportions.

Radish is incompatible with: milk, banana and raisin.

Yogurt is incompatible with: milk, sour fruits, melons, hot drinks, meat, fish, mango, starch and cheese.

Eggs are incompatible with: milk, meat, yogurt, melons, cheese, fish and banana.

Mango is incompatible with: yogurt, cheese and cucumber.

Corn is incompatible with: dates, raisins and banana.

Lemon is incompatible with: yogurt, milk, cucumber and tomato.

Potato, tomato, eggplant (nightshades) are incompatible with: yogurt, milk, melon, and cucumber.

<u>Remember</u>: *Diet changes according to constitution, season, age and diseases.*

••••••••••••••••

RECOMMENDED READING

AYURVEDA, THE SCIENCE OF SELF-HEALING
Dr. Vasant Lad
Lotus Press, 1984

THE AYURVEDIC COOKBOOK
Amadea Morningstar with Urmila Desai
Lotus Press, 1990

••••••••••••••••

11

OSTEOPATHY
Harold I. Magoun, Jr., DO, FAAO, DO Ed. (Hon*)*

·················

There is no form of physical mechanotherapy so near in accord with nature's measures as correctly given Osteopathic adjustments.

EDGAR CAYCE
Reading 1158 - 31

A disturbed artery marks the beginning to an hour and a minute when disease begins to sow its seeds of destruction in the human body. The rule of the artery must be absolute, universal and unobstructed, or disease will be the result.

Andrew Taylor Still, DO
Founder of Osteopathy

Harold I. Magoun, Jr., DO, FAAO, DO Ed. (Hon), has practiced Osteopathy for over 50 years. His father, Harold Magoun, Sr., DO, FAAO., and his mother Helen C. Magoun, DO, met in the early 20s while they were students at the American School of Osteopathy, Kirksville, Missouri. (The school is now known as the Kirksville College of Osteopathic Medicine). During World War II, Dr. Magoun, Jr. received his pre-medical training at Southern Methodist University, Dallas, Texas. He continued his studies and graduated from Kirksville College of Osteopathic Medicine. In 1950 he interned at Rocky Mountain Osteopathic Hospital, Denver, Colorado, and has practiced in Denver ever since. He is Board Certified in Osteopathic Manipulative Medicine. During 1981-1982, he served as President of the American Academy of Osteopathy. He has also served as a member of the Board of Directors of the Cranial Academy. Dr. Magoun earned a Fellowship in the Academy of Osteopathy (F.A.A.O) and is on the Academy's Bureau of Experts. He is also a member of the American Osteopathic Association, the American Academy of Osteopathy, the Cranial Academy, the Colorado Society of Osteopathic Medicine, and the Rocky Mountain Academy of Osteopathy, which he founded in 1992. Dr. Magoun has taught many students, interns and residents at Osteopathic Colleges and Osteopathic programs throughout the United States, Canada, and Germany. He was awarded a Doctor of Osteopathic Education, honorary degree, from Kirksville College of Osteopathic Medicine, on June 3, 2000.

To find health should be the object of the doctor;
Anyone can find disease.

Andrew Taylor Still, DO,
Founder of Osteopathy

The Osteopath, palpates the body to ascertain diverse and
subtle physical, emotional, mental and spiritual complexities
written in the tissues of the patient's body. It is the Osteopath's
job to interpret the significance of the findings and apply
Osteopathic manipulation according to the individual's needs,
to help the patient balance their body, mind, and spirit.

Ralph Thieme, DO,
Member of Teaching Faculty
University of New England
College of Osteopathic Medicine

121

OSTEOPATHY
Interview with Dr. Harold I. Magoun, Jr.,
DO, FAAO, DO Ed. (Hon)

Bette: What does the word "*Osteopathy*" mean?

Dr. Magoun: Dr. Andrew Still, the founder of Osteopathy, coined the word from two Greek words: "*Osteo*" meaning bone and "*pathos*" meaning disease or ill health as a result of malfunction of the bones. Osteopathy is a system of health care that utilizes the body's inherent ability to heal itself by correcting function and thereby improving blood in nerve supply. Osteopaths take a holistic approach of considering the person as a whole rather then focusing on individual organs or systems.

Bette: In your recent book *Structured Healing,* you listed four Osteopathic tenets applied by traditional Osteopaths to be utilized when seeking optimum or high-quality health.

Dr. Magoun: The four tenets you are speaking about are:

(1) Each of us is a unit composed of mind, body and spirit; each part is inter-dependent in maximizing true health; (2) within our bodies, we all have self-healing and self-regulating mechanisms that direct our bodies toward health when given essential materials and support; (3) the body's structure determines how our body functions. Likewise, functional demands on the body can modify its structure; (4) and rational approaches to maximize health involve considering and applying the three other Osteopathic tenets mentioned.

Bette: What is the difference between traditional Osteopathy and non-traditional Osteopathy?

Dr. Magoun: Traditional Osteopathy is what Dr. Andrew Still practiced, getting away from medicine in favor of using manipulation. Those of us who are members of the American Academy of Osteopathy are traditional Osteopaths. Modern Osteopathy is getting in line with traditional medicine, which, in my opinion, is a big mistake. This is an enormous problem because much of the hierarchy of the American Osteopathic Association wants to be recognized with traditional medicine which focuses on certain areas of particular systems. That is exactly what Dr. Still wanted to get away from. Many modern MDs do what they call manual medicine, which is manipulation. These days, all major forms of manipulations, whether done by MDs, chiropractors or physical therapists, originated from the Osteopathic profession.

Bette: On the cover of your book there is a picture of the Pyramids. Why did you choose the Pyramids as an illustration?

Dr. Magoun: The book's cover is symbolically illustrated with the Egyptian Pyramids because to me they are the most famous structures in the world. And the roots of medicine go back to ancient Egypt, so the pyramids seemed an apropos symbol for *Structured Healing*. My book educates the reader in 3 sections: the first section is about how people can improve their health by structuring their lives through nutrition, exercise, mental health, avoiding harmful substances and coping with the environment; section two is on the structure-function relationship of the human body, developing Dr. Still's philosophy, and the development and growth of the Osteopathic profession; and the third section is on managed or structured health care and how it has affected our well-being regarding the human body. The more rigid the structure, the less functional it is.

Bette: When a patient comes to an Osteopaths office, what happens?

Dr. Magoun: That would depend on which Osteopath you went to. Because we are fully licensed to practice medicine, some Osteopaths just practice medicine. If you went to one of those, he/she might ask for an x-ray, or put you on an anti-inflammatory. A true Osteopath would take your history, do a thorough structural examination, which reveals what is going on inside the body, and then would prescribe a particular treatment.

Bette: What type of treatments could you choose from?

Dr. Magoun: There are many different types of Osteopathic manipulations that are appropriate for various conditions, regardless of what the situation is or how critically ill a patient is.

Bette: Manipulation?

Dr. Magoun: Pertaining to Osteopathy, manipulation means a hands-on contact with the tissues. We implement manipulation to adjust the tissues, which includes bones, ligaments, muscles and fascia, and work on the fluids of the body. There are techniques to affect lymphatic fluids, venous fluids and the cerebral spinal fluids. That is all termed manipulation. With a very light manipulation style, we can relieve tensions in the fascias in the body.

Bette: Is fascia that white sinew that you see on a cut of meat in the supermarket?

Dr. Magoun: Yes. That's the sheath of connective tissue which keeps our internal organs enclosed. If all the functional tissues in the body were dissolved, and only the fascia remained, you would still have the full form of the body.

Bette: Are there different light and strong manipulation styles?

Dr. Magoun: We use various gentle procedures to relieve strain in the ligaments that limit the motion of joints; all joints are fashioned with ligaments. For ambulant patients we can use more vigorous techniques. We also have muscular methods called Muscle Energy developed by Dr. Fred Mitchell back in the 60s. Counter strain is another maneuver; it was developed by Dr. Larry Jones at about the same time. The procedure involves positioning the patient in the stance they were in when the strain occurred, holding it there for 90 seconds to allow relaxation of the muscles, and then very slowly returning it to normal. There is also a technique called High Velocity where you find a joint that is restricted, reposition it in a more normal pose and apply a light thrust to restore its normal motion. This is a well-known type of manipulation.

Bette: Is High Velocity what chiropractors employ?

Dr. Magoun: It has been copied by other professions, particularly chiropractic. But they tend to use too much force which can injure people. When it's done properly, High Velocity thrust is a very effective technique.

Bette: Does thrust mean the movement that causes that cracking sound of the bones?

Dr. Magoun: Yes. When you apply a thrust like that, and you separate the joints, you get a momentary vacuum which creates that popping sound.

Bette: What is the difference between Chiropractic and Osteopathy?

Dr. Magoun: Chiropractors have less training in understanding the anatomy and physiology of the spine, less training in manipulation and they don't have the medical training that Osteopaths receive.

***Bette*:** Are there other Osteopathic procedures?

***Dr. Magoun*:** Probably the most significant addition is the cranial concept developed by Dr. William Sutherland in the 30s and 40s. This approach can be applied to all of the tissues in the body, but is primarily focused on the cranium and sacrum, which are related through the attachment of the thick membrane that coves the brain and spinal cord. Problems of the cranium will affect the sacrum and vice-versa. This is what we refer to as the cranio-sacral mechanism.

***Bette*:** What is the cranio-sacral manipulation like?

***Dr. Magoun*:** Cranio-sacral manipulation encompasses a great variety of gentle applications of the hands to the skull (composed of 22 cranial bones which are moveable and pliable) and the sacrum (tail bone which is closely related to the cranium through the attachments of the dura mater). The gentle application of hands ascertains any distortion of the bony components, any changes in the tensions in the membranes which surround and protect the brain and spinal cord, and any alterations in the fluctuation of the cerebro-spinal fluid. Many different procedures are then possible to correct any abnormalities found. These procedures are applicable from newborns to the most elderly.

***Bette*:** Do you prescribe home exercises to your patients?

***Dr. Magoun*:** I give my patients advice about exercise, nutrition, posture and lifestyle, because all of these components are involved in the patient getting better. This really goes back to the Hippocratic philosophy. Hippocrates advocated lifestyle, nutrition, exercise and forms of manipulation which were done back then, but have been lost.

***Bette*:** Do you refer your patients to other practitioners for complementary care?

***Dr. Magoun*:** I sometimes advise patients to get massage therapy, rolfing, physical therapy or acupuncture. For critical neurological problems, I have a neuro-surgeon that I refer patients to. I have been in just a manipulative practice for over 50 years, so I don't see many acute medical problems. We do have some board certified family practitioners in Denver, so if it is a medical problem that I don't think I can handle, I refer it to someone else.

***Bette*:** Out of a total of over 14,000 readings that Edgar Cayce conducted, he recommended Osteopathy over 6000 times. Are you familiar with his readings?

Dr. Magoun: I am well-acquainted with the readings. I utilize many of Mr. Cayce's suggestions in my practice, including hot castor oil packs. They work very well for muscular aches and pains. Usually I use the packs with a hot water bottle or heating pad with plastic between to contain the oil.

Bette: Why do you think Cayce chose Osteopathy so many times in preference to other healing modalities?

Dr. Magoun: Cayce recognized how much Osteopathy deals with natural laws of healing. Even though we are a minority profession, we are in an ideal situation. Osteopaths are fully licensed to practice medicine. There are many instances where you need to control pain or other symptoms. We can prescribe medication when necessary. But if you do only that, you are just treating symptoms. However, if you are also working with Osteopathic manipulations to remove the cause of the problem then you are doing a better service to your patient.

Bette: Do you equate the human nervous system to an electrical wiring system?

Dr. Magoun: It's a great deal more intricate then that. The human nervous system is more comparable to a computer with minute connections and possibilities of malfunction from many different standpoints: mechanical problems, chemical problems, inflammatory problems, and numerous other things that can affect human nervous system functioning.

Bette: Cayce spoke about harmony in the nervous system as strategic to good health. Why is this necessary?

Dr. Magoun: It is absolutely essential. The nervous system is closely related to the endocrine system - hormones and enzymes - so much so that we refer to it as the neuroendocrine system. Normalizing body structure will help the body normalize those functions. Dr. Still stressed normalizing blood and nerve supply.

Bette: Can moving a joint bring the nervous system into balance?

Dr. Magoun: There is a tremendous amount of feedback into the central nervous system from every joint in the body. This is particularly so for the spinal joints in regard to feedback to the voluntary nervous system and the involuntary nervous system as well, which controls all of the involuntary functions. It is very important to correct disturbances in these areas so the body will be able to heal itself.

***Bette*:** What are the involuntary functions you are speaking about?

***Dr. Magoun*:** Our nervous system is divided into two main parts: the voluntary and the involuntary. And each of those is subdivided. In the voluntary you have the sensory side which gives you pain, touch and temperature. And you have the motor side which gives you voluntary actions. The involuntary system is divided into the sympathetic and the parasympathetic.

***Bette*:** For many years they talked about those two systems working synergistically.

***Dr. Magoun*:** They don't. They are pretty much independent. The sympathetic nervous system is referred to commonly as the "fight or flight" mechanism. It speeds up the heart when you are frightened or angry, dilates the pupils, increases heart rate, shuts down the sphincters and controls circulation. Because of the way the sympathetic nervous system operates chemically, it's very apt to overreact to situations. Many chronic pain problems and casualties are due to overactivity in the sympathetic nervous system. Our para sympathetic nervous system comes mainly through the vagus nerve and down through the base of the skull. It controls the homeostasis of the body regulating the glandular function, heart rate, kidney function and muscular function that moves through the stomach and bowels.

***Bette*:** If either of these nervous systems gets out of balance what happens?

***Dr. Magoun*:** It has a very drastic effect on one's body, mind and spirit.

***Bette*:** When you determine that a patient has psychological problems do you refer them to counseling?

***Dr. Magoun*:** Sometimes. But with nervous and mental problems there are always structural components. A good many years ago, one of Dr. Andrew Still's early students, Dr. Arthur Hilldreth, found that there was a close relationship between restriction of the first cervical, which is the first vertebrae in the neck and the fourth thoracic, which is the fourth one down below the shoulders, in depression. This is known as the Hilldreth Lesion. I have found this to be consistently accurate. Dr. Hilldreth became interested in nervous and mental disorders. At the time of WWI, he founded the Macon, Missouri, Still-Hilldreth Osteopathic Sanitarium, which operated for many years.

***Bette*:** Have clinical studies continued on the relationship between structure and mental disorders?

Dr. Magoun: Back in the 60s Dr.'s John and Rachel Woods, husband and wife who were very accomplished in cranial manipulation, spent a year at Still-Hilldreth studying the relationship between nervous and mental diseases and the cranial concept. They thought they might find a connection between certain strain patterns and diseases like schizophrenia or manic depression; but they didn't. What they found was a very consistent lowering of the cranial rhythmic impulse. This means movement in the brain and fluctuation of the cerebro-spinal fluid, usually 10 or 12 cycles per minute in normal patients. In severe and nervous mental diseases they discovered a markedly decreased rate, sometimes 4, 5 or 6 cycles per minute.

Bette: Did these cases respond to Osteopathic treatment?

Dr. Magoun: They did. And these patients also usually needed improved nutrition. Sometimes counseling helped too. But all of these patients with nervous and mental diseases had structural problems.

Bette: Did the structural problem precede the mental disorder?

Dr. Magoun: More than likely. If a patient is depressed and in chronic pain, the typical psychiatric diagnosis is that the pain is due to the depression. But usually, because the patient is in chronic pain and unable to work or do things that they normally would do, they become depressed.

Bette: What scientific experiments have been conducted to support the vital role of the nervous system and the part that Osteopathy plays in effectively influencing the body?

Dr. Magoun: The first really scientific research was done at the turn of the century by Dr. Louisa Burns. She had a laboratory in Los Angeles where she did her research, which was published in four volumes. However, not much subsequent scientific study was done for many years. This provoked constant criticism from the medical profession, even though Osteopathy was very successful clinically. Then, in the 40s, Dr. Denslow, a physician on the staff of the Kirksville College of Osteopathy and Surgery Medical College, started doing more scientific research. In 1945, the College hired researcher, I.M. Korr, Ph.D. A year later, I enrolled at that college, and Dr. Korr was my physiology professor. Dr. Korr and his associates did a great variety of work on the neuro-musculo-skeletal system. They proved how the body functions, and substantiated Dr. Still's principles. Dr. Korr's accomplishments have been validated by scientists world-wide. There also has been a tremendous amount of research at Kirksville College, Michigan State University and at the Texas Osteopathic College of Medicine. Even international scientists have done significant work showing that the Osteopathic concept is a very solid phenomena based on the way the body functions.

Bette: Was Osteopathy accepted during its early years?

Dr. Magoun: The whole history of medicine has been one of rejection of new ideas. Osteopathy was no exception. Dr. Still was an MD during the Civil War. He was dissatisfied with the practice of medicine. He was concerned for the large number of morphine addicts arising from the customary prescription of morphine to relieve pain. His experiments with manual methods proved to be quite effective.

Bette: Shouldn't that have been enough to change the standard medical practices of the day?

Dr. Magoun: It wasn't. Changes, even for the better, did not come easily. During the Civil War all doctors were called into service. When Dr. Still returned from the battle, he discovered that fewer children had died while the doctors were away. It seemed strange, but physicians at the time used Calomel, which was chloride of mercury, a deadly poison. The death of three of his own children to spinal meningitis caused Dr. Still to launch into an intense study of anatomy. He examined his patients meticulously, in an effort to improve the practice of medicine, surgery and obstetrics. Although his manual treatments for complaints about tightness, inflammation and soreness countered pain, his ideas were rejected by the medical community.

Bette: Is that the reason he started a new school of medicine?

Dr. Magoun: That was the impetus when, on June 22, 1874, he announced a new school of medicine called Osteopathy. Within a few years he became world famous. His practice, in Kirksville, Missouri, drew huge crowds wanting to be treated by him. In response, the Wabash Railroad had to put extra trains on from St. Louis to Kirksville. Dr. Still could not handle teaching the large numbers of people who wanted to learn Osteopathy. So he opened the first college of Osteopathy in 1892. His initial class consisted of 18 students, but within a few years the college was seating 160, and then 300, 400 and 500 students. It expanded very rapidly.

Bette: How many Osteopathic colleges exist today?

Dr. Magoun: There are 19. They all teach the same basic Osteopathic principles. Some students go to Osteopathic college not expecting to practice Osteopathy; instead, they plan to use it as a door to medicine, which is too bad.

Bette: How can a person find a competent traditional Osteopath to go to?

Dr. Magoun: The best reference is through the American Academy of Osteopathy. The medical profession has many subdivisions: surgeons, obstetricians, psychiatrists, proctologists, sports medicine, rhumatologists. Members of the American Academy of Osteopathy specialize in manipulation. Their offices are located in Indianapolis; they have a website and an email address.

Bette: When a new patient comes to your office, do you take x-rays?

Dr. Magoun: There are many unnecessary x-rays and MRIs done. However, some Osteopaths do indulge in this. But those of us trained to examine the tissues very often don't need x-rays. In my case, as a certified specialist, patients that I see have often already been x-rayed, gone through MRIs , lab tests and what-not, and the problem still hasn't been found. Many of the functional changes causing disease, pain, discomfort and structural changes, don't show up on an x-ray. But you can find it with a palpatory sense when examining the tissues. Very often, I use x-ray or MRI to rule out certain serious things. But I don't routinely x-ray my patients.

Bette: Palpatory means touch?

Dr. Magoun: Sense of touch.

Bette: And you take an oral history which gives you information that you need on how to treat the patient?

Dr. Magoun: That's right. And very often taking an oral history can be shorter than a regular MDs because our palpatory findings tell us a lot of things that sometimes a patient hasn't revealed. Often we find evidence of a problem that might be causing symptoms. When we ask the patient about this, they may say, "Oh, yes, I have been having problems with my stomach!", or whatever the discovered symptomatic problem is.

Bette: Are you saying that while you are doing a palpatory examination you can tell what problems the patient is probably suffering from?

Dr. Magoun: Yes. I can tell if a patient has sustained injuries, is not eating properly, has diabetes, is experiencing stress, has a heart problem or is an alcoholic, amongst other things. This is an art that flourished with some of the medical profession at one time. The thing that made the Mayo Institute so outstanding was that they were great at physical diagnosis. They palpated their patients, but they don't do that any more.

Bette: Why did they stop palpating?

Dr. Magoun: They were swayed by modern technology. MRIs, ultra sound and things like that have taken them away from palpating examinations. It's too bad because it increases the cost of medicine. Also, doctors don't know what they are looking for, so they depend on MRIs and laboratory tests to tell them. A number of years ago a laboratory technician told me that her pet peeve was doing lab work and having the doctor leaning in the doorway waiting for her to make a diagnosis.

Bette: So you believe the preference for practicing as a regular MD, rather than as an Osteopath, is because it's easier?

Dr. Magoun: It's hard work giving Osteopathic treatments and a lot easier to give shots or prescriptions. And some people don't appreciate what the Osteopathic concept has to offer for health care. It helps to have a mechanical aptitude to be a good Osteopath.

Bette: The readings compare what a properly done Osteopathic manipulation does for the body to what a piano tuner can do for a piano. What success stories can you relate about "fine tuning" the body with Osteopathic manipulation to rid a patient of pain or disease?

Dr. Magoun: This happens almost every day. The body will heal if given the chance to do so. I don't think there is any profession like Osteopathy that has a richer tradition of near miraculous cures. One of the most dramatic occurrences was with a two year old named Fred Mitchell, Jr. The child was badly burned in a serious fire in the Mitchell's Chattanooga, Tennessee home. Although he received medical care he kept sinking lower and lower, until finally his kidneys shut down. Physicians informed the little boy's parents that it would be a matter of hours before death claimed the child. The Mitchell's knew of an Osteopath named Dr. Short, who practiced in Chattanooga. His brother-in-law, Dr. Chapman, had discovered very important neuro-lymphatic reflexes throughout the body known as Chapman's Reflexes. For every inflammatory problem in the body there is a specific Chapman Reflex. Dr. Short was called in and he worked on the Chapman's Reflexes in the child's kidneys, adrenals, and liver to support his metabolism. Within an hour of Osteopathic manipulation the little boy's kidneys began functioning again, and he lived. Mr. Mitchell was so impressed with his son's recovery that he sold his business, studied Osteopathy and came up with the Muscle Energy concept of Osteopathic treatment. Fred, Jr. grew up, followed in his father's footsteps and also became an Osteopath. He is now on the faculty of our Michigan State College of Osteopathic Medicine.

Bette: What is the Muscle Energy concept?

Dr. Magoun: This is where you have the patient apply their own muscular effort during treatment. There are three applications: Isometric where the operator applies the same force as the patient so there is no motion involved; there's an Isotonic where the operator applies a little less force than the patient and this is to strengthen muscles; and there's an Isolitic where the operator applies a greater force than the patient to stretch stiff muscles. All three applications are applicable where there is muscle tissue. Muscle Energy techniques are a wonderful addition to the Osteopathy.

Bette: How many Osteopaths are currently in practice?

Dr. Magoun: There are 45,000 Osteopathic physicians presently practicing. And better than 20% of Armed Forces Medical Corp are Osteopaths. While medical schools are cutting back, because there is a surplus of doctors in metropolitan areas, we are expanding because of a greater demand for Osteopathic services.

Bette: What is a facilitated segment?

Dr. Magoun: It is an irritated segment of the spinal cord, created by restriction of the spinal joints at that segmental level, causing over-activity of the neuro-muscular reflexes. This was first described by IM Korr, Ph.D., at Kirksville.

Bette: Are there Osteopathic manipulations that can be done at home to correct a facilitated segment?

Dr. Magoun: For a person in an acute asthmatic attack, a deep pressure on either side of the fourth thoracic, which is four segments down from the base of the neck, will relieve the facilitated segment that is causing the bronchial constriction and ease breathing. This technique was developed by Dr. Perrin T. Wilson, a well-known Osteopath who was my father's family physician. Another very dramatic technique is pressure on either side of the fifth lumbar, which is the lowest vertebrae in the back, to ease menstrual cramps. Women suffering this discomfort usually have mechanical problems in the lower back. They get congestion in the uterus during their period, and the uterus cramps down to expel the clots. That's very painful. The muscle spasm will be eased instantly with applied pressure on either side of the fifth lumbar.

Bette: Do you apply the pressure with your thumbs?

Dr. Magoun: I use the side of my index finger and thumb. On my first date with my ex-wife, we went to see a play. She was squirming in her seat and was obviously in some distress. I asked her what was wrong and she told me she was having cramps. So I reached over behind her and applied that pressure to the sides of her fifth lumbar; in a minute she was comfortable.

Bette: The Cayce readings and medical science show a direct relationship between our spine segments and our internal organs. Can you predict a disease that has not yet surfaced by examining the condition of the spine?

Dr. Magoun: Yes. This is the way the human nervous system is set up, particularly through the sympathetic nervous system. It arises through two trunks on either side of the thoracic spine, which is the rib area. The classic text on this subject, "Symptoms of Visceral Disease", was written by Dr. Pottinger, an MD. He explained this segmental innervation and the reflexes which are all mapped out from the thyroid gland, which is at the first thoracic, to the heart around the third thoracic, the bronchial at the fourth thoracic, the stomach at the sixth and seventh thoracic, pancreas 7th and 8th and the liver at the ninth thoracic, etc

Bette: You use these reflexes in the spine for diagnosis?

Dr. Magoun: Yes, to help diagnose and treat an ailment that has not yet surfaced. You cannot predict the time that such an episode may take place, only the probability. Because of what was considered his radical ideas at the time, Pottinger was drummed out of the medical corps. Ten years later, when they discovered that he was right, he was brought back with honors. Dr. Pottinger's text was one that we used when I was in Osteopathic school 50 years ago.

Bette: Can most conditions be treated in one session?

Dr. Magoun: If the problem is something recent, yes. But if it's a long term problem, or an organic disease of some kind or an old injury, it takes time. And very often you have to educate your patient. If they are used to taking a pain pill that works in 20 minutes and lasts for 4 hours, sometimes they expect the same thing from manipulation. It does not work that way with Osteopathic treatment; it takes more time.

Bette: Is manipulation painful?

Dr. Magoun: It can be uncomfortable at times, but should never be painful if done properly.

Bette: Do you prescribe stress reduction and meditation to your patients?

Dr. Magoun: Absolutely. And also Yoga - everything but the headstand.

Bette: How much importance do you place on the role of nutrition in a person's overall health?

Dr. Magoun: It is of upmost importance. I am very knowledgeable about nutrition. At one time I had a nutritionist in my office. But not enough patients availed themselves of it. My mother came from a tubercular family; she had TB of the kidneys and was bedridden for many years. Her doctors did not expect her to live. When I was in Osteopathic school, my parents learned about Adelle Davis, one of the early nutritionists in California. They got my mother on Adelle Davis' nutritional program, which enabled her to lead a normal life. My mother died at age 79. I, too, got on a good nutritional program when I got out of Osteopathic school 50 years ago. Good nutrition is one of the reasons that I have never lost a day from the office due to sickness in 50 years of practice.

Bette: What does your diet consist of?

Dr. Magoun: High protein, no refined carbohydrates, and vitamin and mineral supplements. The main part of my diet is meat, fish, seafood, colored vegetables and whole grains. I think there is a lot of validity to what Dr. Peter D'Adamo said in his book *Eat Right For Your Blood Type*. I follow most of his advice and don't have any noticeable allergies. As a type "O", I'm not supposed to drink milk. I took note of that because I was a bottle baby and did not tolerate cow's milk. I was raised on goat's milk; type "Os" can't tolerate dairy products. I know that the more positive things you bring into your lifestyle, the healthier you will be.

Bette: Would you say that accenting the positive is a key to staying healthy?

Dr. Magoun: The best preventative medicine of all is keeping yourself healthy through good nutrition, adequate fluid intake, avoiding harmful substances, exercise, rest, a positive attitude, stress reduction techniques like meditation, and keeping the body healthy structurally to allow it to function normally. Exercise will help improve the structure-function relationship of the body, but the best thing is regular Osteopathic treatment.

••••••••••••••••

The Osteopath reasons, if he reasons at all,
that order and health are inseparable, that when
order in all parts is found, disease cannot prevail.

Andrew Still, DO
Founder of Osteopathy

••••••••••••••••

For further information about Osteopathy contact:

American Academy of Osteopathy
3500 De Pauw Boulevard., Suite 1080
Indianapolis, IN 46268
Website: http//www.academyofosteopathy.org

The Cranial Academy
8202 Clearvista Parkway, #9-D
Indianapolis, IN 46256
(317) 594-0411
Email: cranacad@aol.com

••••••••••••••••

RECOMMENDED READING

STRUCTURED HEALING
Harold I. Magoun, Jr., DO, F.A.S.., DO Ed. (Hon)
Full Spectrum Arts, Inc., 2001

LET'S GET WELL
Adelle Davis
Harcourt Brace & Co., 1965

SPONTANEOUS HEALING:
How to Discover and Enhance Your Body's
Natural Ability to Maintain and Heal Itself
Andrew Weil, MD
Ivy Books, 2000

················

Then the science of Osteopathy is not merely the punching
in a certain segment or the cracking of the bones, but it is the
keeping of a balance - by the touch - between the sympathetic
and the cerebrospinal system! That is real Osteopathy!

Edgar Cayce
Reading 1158-24

12

BIOLOGICAL DENTISTRY
A HOLISTIC APPROACH
Marilyn K. Jones, DDS

••••••••••••••••

*Once cavities have developed, the readings recommend
filling them with something other than heavy metals, like gold.*

Eric Mein, MD
From: *KEYS TO HEALTH*

---

*The removal of silver mercury amalgam fillings
should be avoided during pregnancy.*

Marilyn K. Jones, DDS
Holistic Dentist

Marilyn K. Jones, DDS., graduated from the University of Texas Dental
Branch, Houston, Texas. She continued her studies in cosmetic and restorative
dentistry, occlusion (the way the upper and lower teeth fit together), TMJ
(temporomandibular (jaw) joint function), periodontal (gum) disease, and
nutrition. Dr. Jones completed a residency in Periodontics at the University of
Texas Dental Branch. She is a member of the Academy of General Dentistry
and has a holistic general dental practice in Houston, Texas. Dr. Jones practices
clinical nutrition using non-invasive testing methods along with biological
dentistry which employs the latest technologies and bioenergetic medicines.

*I educate my patients on how to prevent many
dental problems naturally by building the immune
system through diet, exercise and a positive attitude.*

Marilyn K. Jones, DDS
Holistic Dentist

•••••••••••••••••

BIOLOGICAL DENTISTRY
Marilyn Jones, DDS

The first time I met holistic dentist Dr. Marilyn Jones was at the Houstonian, a Houston, Texas health club. We were both lifting weights in front of the mirrored gym wall. Between sets, a young pregnant woman resting on a weight lifting bench was telling Dr. Jones about her oral problems. "My gums are very sensitive and bleed so easily, Marilyn."

"Your gum tissues are hypersensitive because of hormonal changes that occur during pregnancy," Dr. Jones answered. "And toxins from bacteria in plaque and broken down white blood cells contribute to gingivitis. That's the disease that causes inflammation of the gums."

I was interested in the conversation because my daughter was pregnant. She, too, was complaining about sensitive gums. And she also needed a filling in a front tooth.

"Gum disease indicates that the permeability of cell membranes has changed and fluids and minerals have leaked out," Dr. Jones explained. "This is an ideal environment for bacteria to cause inflammation and infection around the tooth."

"Is it true that babies born to women with gingivitis are generally below normal birth weight?" inquired the young woman.

"That is what scientific studies indicate," Dr. Jones replied. "But the good news is that foods rich in folic acid, like organ meats, molasses and fermented soy tempeh help eliminate toxins and irritants from plaque."

I joined in on the conversation, "Would it be safe for my pregnant daughter to have an old filling replaced?"

Dr. Jones said that usually all she recommends during pregnancy is dental cleaning every three months, and regular brushing and flossing. She also suggests alternative cleaning techniques like using a rubber tip stimulator followed with an irrigator filled with water, baking soda and 3% Hydrogen Peroxide. Dr. Jones said that pregnant women should avoid x-rays, anesthetics, and removal of old or the placement of new silver-amalgam fillings. She suggested that if it can be planned, amalgam fillings should be removed prior to pregnancy, because silver-amalgams contain silver, tin, zinc, copper and 50% mercury, a highly toxic substance. Scientific research has linked mercury to: the possible cause of birth defects, infertility, multiple sclerosis, Alzheimer's disease, Hodgkin's disease, chronic fatigue syndrome, all autoimmune disorders, increased salivation, indigestion, sporadic blurring of vision, chills, a metallic taste in the mouth, sleep disorders, tinnitus, irritability and many other maladies.

I learned that mercury can be concentrated in sperm, and passed on to the fertilized embryo. Mercury in a pregnant woman's system will be absorbed by the fetus, which becomes a dump for toxins and heavy metals from the mother's body. However, most mercury is slowly excreted through the kidneys, colon, sweat, bile, milk and other body secretions. Silver mercury amalgam fillings leak mercury when a person consumes hot fluids. The body absorbs mercury and, according to an individual's tolerance for it, can cause poisoning.

She explained that when a patient has a silver mercury amalgam removed, she follows a protocol established by the International Academy of Oral Medicine and Toxicology. The procedure begins by testing the amalgam for negative charges. Then she removes the quadrant with the highest negative charge first, followed by the quadrant with the second highest negative charge, and so forth, down to zero. After all negative charges are out, the highest positive charge is removed until the removal process is down to zero. Amalgams are never removed on the 7th day of the cycle (i.e. 7, 14, 21, 28) because the immune system cycles down at that time.

Dr. Jones said that she wears a respirator and has an in-room filter to cut down on exposure to mercury when she removes amalgam. To prevent the patient from swallowing silver mercury amalgam, a rubber dam is stretched across the patient's mouth. A rubber dam has holes poked into it for the teeth to stick through. While Dr. Jones works on a patient she uses a water spray to keep the vapor down. The patient's nose is covered and kept ventilated so mercury vapors are not trapped in the nostrils. High speed evacuation is implemented to rapidly remove pieces of amalgam. After the rubber dam is removed, the patient's mouth is rinsed well. These precautions may minimize mercury absorption into the body. Dr. Jones said that prior to a procedure, all materials used for any dental work that she performs, including replacement of silver mercury amalgams, are tested for patient biocompatibility.

Nutritional support is vital before and after the removal of silver-amalgam fillings. Dr. Jones explained that dietary aids, and whole food supplements from organic plants and animals, help strengthen the immune system and protect the body from mercury poisoning. Foods that detoxify are: fruit pectin, green beans, zucchini, parsley, celery, cilantro, garlic, and meals containing iron, calcium, amino acids, sulfur, zinc, selenium, B-complex and vitamin C. "Homeopathic medicines and herbs have also been successfully used in mercury detoxification," she said. "Blue Green Algae is another detoxifier. But it may have bacteria and heavy metals like mercury in it, due to its source: the ocean."

Some States have even issued fish and drinking water advisories because of chemical contamination in water polluted with pesticides, industrial wastes, and high mercury content in fish, such as tuna and swordfish. "These fish should not be eaten, particularly during pregnancy," Dr. Jones warned. She also mentioned other things containing mercury that pregnant women should avoid: contact lens solution, Preparation H, mercurochrome, merthiolate, topical fungicide (yellow mercuric oxide), cosmetics (lip gloss, mascara), and water base paints (phenyl mercuric propionate) containing mercury compounds.

Since my daughter was in her second trimester, Dr. Jones felt that the baby would be less susceptible to dental treatment that my daughter received. If the tooth decay was in an area of my daughter's mouth that did not have an old filling in it, Dr. Jones said she could probably take care of it without placing amalgams or using a drill. And if my daughter was not too sensitive, the work could be done without the use of anesthetics. Instead, the painless air abrasion technique, which works like a high powered car wash spray, would spread a powder on the tooth to eliminate the decay. A composite would then be bonded where the decay was removed. She explained that this method worked well on small areas of decay. For larger areas she uses anesthetic, then drills and finishes up with air abrasion.

Dr. Jones pointed out that decay usually indicates degeneration in the body, a low blood phosphorus level and a carbohydrate metabolism that is out of balance. Sugar not only causes decay on the surface of the teeth, but it also is responsible for a systemic reaction that reduces the hydrostatic pressure inside the tooth. "Most of the time, after examining a patient's nutrition, I recommend a higher protein diet than they normally consume," she said. "That is because carbohydrates are easier to come by. Generally, protein is what we need more of."

"Do you recommend breast feeding?" I asked.

"Absolutely, even up to two years of age, because breast milk is superior to commercial formulas and powdered milk," she told me. "Breast milk contains live enzymes and calcium that can easily assimilate in a baby's body for proper jaw and tooth formation." She cautioned anyone planning to breast feed to be particularly careful about mercury exposure. Until the baby is weaned, mercury is absorbed into breast milk. An infant cannot excrete mercury from its body.

"My education is continuous so I am always well informed about state of the art care for my patients," said Dr. Jones. She studies with experts like Dr. Hal Huggins, a dental surgeon who devotes his practice to patients suffering from mercury toxicity and autoimmune diseases. His clinic, in Colorado Springs, Colorado, focuses on dentistry, medicine, nutrition, psychology and other healing arts. Dr. Huggins wrote *It's All in Your Head*, a New York Times Best Seller book about scientific evidence linking mercury exposure to degenerative disease and other ailments.

Dr. Voll is another dental expert with whom Dr. Jones did a course of study. He taught her that teeth are like a blueprint of the body. His research validated the relationship between teeth and specific acupuncture meridians, using an electro-acupuncture Biofeedback technique.

Early Chinese physicians discovered that blocked energy produced illness. They concluded that the solution was to balance energies referred to as the yin and the yang. They found that health could be restored to the body systems by stimulating the natural healing energy of the body known as the Qi (pronounced "chee"). This was accomplished through manipulation of acupuncture needles, or with the application of pressure (Acupressure) along meridians, the pathways of more than one-thousand energy points (Acupoints) just below the surface of the skin. Certain meridians directly affect specific organs (i.e. heart, lungs, spleen, etc.) and other parts of the anatomy. Each tooth lies in a meridian and has an energy compatible with the meridian that influences an organ, nerves, vertebrae, muscles and everything on that organ. According to scientific research, when a tooth is stimulated, a measurable simultaneous energy change occurs in the organ, on the same meridian (from tooth to organ) and vice versa (from organ to tooth). "Teeth are energy circuit breakers for the whole body," Dr. Jones informs me.

"I will tell my daughter about what I have learned," I said. I thanked Dr. Jones for the information. All of it was new to me. Our family dentist was still using silver mercury amalgam fillings.

As it turned out, I was treated by Dr. Jones before my daughter was. I made an appointment with her when my wisdom tooth became infected, causing my face to swell up. Anxiously, I waited for my turn in Dr. Jones' office, wondering if I was in store for more pain than I was already experiencing. The tense expression on my swollen face reflected itself in the mirror lining one of the office walls. Later I found out that the mirror was deliberately placed on the wall, because healing energy from the third eye, which is invisibly located in the middle of the forehead, hits the mirror and reflects itself back to the patient.

I momentarily took my mind off my discomfort by reading a magazine article about Rev. Willard Fuller, a faith healer from Georgia, practicing the principles of alchemy, the science of mind and body transformation. Rev. Fuller specializes in performing dental miracles that turn silver amalgams to gold. He also fills cavities with a mysterious white substance, properly aligns jaws and straightens and closes spaces between teeth.

When Dr. Jones greeted me, I asked her if she knew about Rev. Fuller. "I would really have to see his dental healing to believe it," I told her. "I have seen it," she informed me. "Rev. Fuller's gold restorations are perfect and much shinier than the gold dentists use." She told me that she had observed Rev. Fuller doing a dental healing on a group of people at a church. "He likes to heal the mouth because people can easily see the changes that take place, as opposed to healing internal organs that are not visible," Dr. Jones explained. She said that Rev. Fuller uses music to transform energy into healing vibrations in the body, mind and spirit. He joins the congregation in singing songs about acceptance and receiving while he and his wife touch everyone who came for a healing. Rev. Fuller always inquires about the condition of each person's teeth and examines everyone with a mouth mirror. He makes notes about things they have forgotten concerning their teeth, or about conditions in their mouth that they did not know existed. "A good test of Rev. Fuller's expertise would be for a dentist to compare a person's dental records with the person's mouth, before a healing. After Rev. Fuller's healing the dentist could contrast the condition of the person's mouth with his/her dental records, and document any changes that occurred," Dr. Jones said.

She spoke about observing a dental healing that Rev. Fuller performed on a man, and the white substance that slowly filled up the man's decayed teeth. Rev. Fuller told Dr. Jones that dental miracles also happen weeks after a healing had occurred. He spoke to her about a woman with ill-fitting dentures who grew new teeth thirteen days after experiencing a healing. "I am on the list to take Rev. Fuller's tooth healing course when he comes back to Houston," Dr. Jones said.

"A dental healing seems incredible," I remarked. Dr. Jones reminded me that the Cayce readings tell us it is physically possible, with the right mental and spiritual attitude, for a body to produce anything which it has produced before, including new teeth or a new limb.

The lighting in her treatment room was subdued and relaxing, and music was softly playing in the background. As she examined my mouth, she told me I would have to wait for treatment until the infection in my wisdom tooth subsided. I had a choice of antibiotics or complementary medicine.

"Antibiotics could kill the good and the bad pathogenic bacteria," she informed me. "You would need to take acidophilus to replace the good bacteria." I decided to take complementary medicine. Dr. Jones prescribed homeopathic medicines, arnica 30, mercurius sol 6 or 30 and pyrogen 30 to reduce the soreness, swelling and infection. She gave me a bottle of a whole food vitamin complex. Her instructions were to take the vitamins every quarter-hour, with a teaspoon of ginger and turmeric, which is a natural antibiotic, until the infection disappeared.

X-rays were necessary to determine the extent of my dental problem. "Eating Miso will help eliminate x-ray radiation from your body," Dr. Jones told me. She also recommended another method for expelling body heat after x-ray exposure. "Take a 30-minute bath in a very hot tub of water containing one pound of baking soda and one pound of ordinary table salt."

After examining my x-rays, Dr. Jones thought it best to extract my wisdom tooth because the infected tooth could not benefit me in any way. She said that once it was removed there would be less stress in my mouth. I felt panicked thinking about a tooth extraction But Dr. Jones assured me that I would be fine. With her hand on my shoulder, she explained that a lot of healing takes place by touch and positive affirmations. "All it takes to prevent discomfort is a little extra preparation by the dentist and the patient." She gave me Rescue Remedy, a homeopathic Bach Flower remedy, for the relief of anxiety and stress. "Would you like me to put you in a trance on the day of the extraction, or would you prefer a recommended psychotherapist to train you in self-hypnosis?" she asked. Dental acupuncture or regular local anesthesia were other options that she offered me. I told her I wanted time to think about my choices.

During the next 24 hours, I followed Dr. Jones' instructions. The pain subsided and the swelling disappeared. She asked me to decide if I really wanted to have my wisdom tooth extracted. If my answer was yes - which it was - I was to assure myself that it was a good decision. Then I was to recite the releasing and grieving exercise she had written down on paper for me. This psychological preparation included my verbal thank you to the tooth for the years of service it had given me, and for all the function it provided: the chewing, the looking good, and the holding of the space with the other teeth. I advised the tooth that its energy had changed, it would be better off somewhere else, and I would be better off without it. I told myself that I was ready to release the tooth for my own good and for the good of the universe.

A few days later I returned to Dr. Jones' office. Thirty minutes before I arrived, I took Arnica 30 and Rescue Remedy, as she had instructed. Although I was still concerned about having my wisdom tooth extracted, I felt less apprehensive in the dental chair then the time before. I told Dr. Jones that I had decided in favor of regular local anesthesia.

She offered me a blanket, which I accepted. Her nurse tucked me into the chair. I felt cozy and comfortable. Soothing music played. It sounded like the rhythmic beat of ocean waves. The subliminal healing message in the music tuned my chakras, the seven energy vortices influencing physical, emotional and spiritual patterns of awareness. Dr. Jones said, "You will be even more relaxed as your heart rhythm slows down to a normal 60 beats a minute in syncopation to the subliminal 60 beats a minute of the music." She explained that during the procedure I would be listening to baroque classical music because that type of music proved to have a healing affect on the body.

With her hand gently placed on my shoulder, she asked me to join her in a prayer for a painless extraction and rapid healing. I closed my eyes and together we prayed, "I release, I release, and send my wisdom tooth off." Dr. Jones said the prayer would help me emotionally and influence the ease of the extraction. I followed her guided visualizations and imagined the tooth coming out and floating off the horizon, until it became a tiny speck that I could no longer see. I saw myself clipping any cord that remained between me and the tooth. And I visualized my body healing the gum and the bone around the extraction.

The nurse placed a pair of green goggles over my eyes. Green is a color that encourages healing. The goggles were also used to protect my eyes from air and water. Dr. Jones rubbed an extract of marigold on my gum to numb the area for the Novocain. Throughout the procedure she repeatedly asked me if I was comfortable. "You will not experience any pain or discomfort," she assured me as the needle entered my gum. She was right. I did not feel the injection, nor did my heart race, as it usually does when I take Novocain, because there was no epinephrine in the local anesthetic.

Dr. Jones said that I was in full control and could stop the procedure at any time. I closed my eyes as she inserted a small tool, resembling pliers, into my mouth. I felt mild pressure but no pain or discomfort. "You are doing fine," she told me as she removed my wisdom tooth. She was so gentle and quick that I did not know the extraction and removal of fibers and infected bone had taken

144

place. When she showed me the wisdom tooth she had removed, I felt an immediate sense of loss and relief. "The procedure has gone very well," she commented. "Allow the raw nerves and gum tissue to heal for twenty-four hours."

Slowly she sat me up, patted my shoulder and reminded me not to touch the area around the extraction. She rubbed Traumeel Ointment on my face over the extraction area. The ointment is a homeopathic preparation used to prevent pain and swelling. Dr. Jones gave me a therapeutic magnet to hold against my face over the uprooted tooth area. The magnet encourages increased blood circulation which brings fresh nutrients to the extraction area and rapidly removes toxins. This process aids the body in healing rapidly. "There will be no post-operative bleeding, swelling or pain," Dr. Jones told me.

Amazingly, the entire procedure was painless, with no side effects during or after the extraction. I drove home, had a soft dinner and, as Dr. Jones had prescribed, took a whole food complex vitamin C, echinachea, and the homeopathic medicine hypericum 6. To avoid irritating the extraction area, I followed her instructions and did not rinse my mouth or brush my teeth. I slept through the night without pain, swelling, bleeding or other discomfort. Three days later I went to the Houstonian Health Club to exercise and lift weights with Dr. Jones. I felt great!

•••••••••••••••••

Dr. Marilyn Jones can be contacted at:

7500 San Felipe Street
Houston, Texas 77063
Phone: 713-785-8677

•••••••••••••••••

•••••••••••••••••

RECOMMENDED READING

IT'S ALL IN YOUR HEAD
Hal A. Huggins, DDS
Avery Publishing Group, 1993

SILVER DENTAL FILLINGS:
The Toxic Time Bomb
Sam Ziff
Aurora Press, Inc., 1984

INFERTILITY AND BIRTH DEFECTS:
Is Mercury From Silver Dental
Fillings a Hidden Cause?
Sam and Michael Ziff
Bio-Probe, Inc., 1988

MERCURY POISONING
FROM DENTAL AMALGAM:
A Hazard to the Human Brain
Patrick Storetebecker, MD
Bio-Probe, Inc., 1986

FOODS THAT HEAL:
A Guide to Understanding and Using
the Healing Powers of Natural Foods
Dr. Bernard Jensen
Putnam Publishing Group, 1988

•••••••••••••••••

For further information contact:

The Foundation for Toxic Free Dentistry
PO Box 580160
Orlando, Florida 32858

DAMS, Inc.
(Dental Amalgam Mercury Syndrome)
PO Box 7249
Minneapolis, MN. 55407
1-800-311-6265

....

*For referrals of practitioners trained
in nutritional medicine contact:*

American College Of Advancement In Medicine
23121 Verdugo Drive, Suite 204
Laguna Hills, CA. 92653
714-583-7666

....

Contact Rev. Willlard Fuller at:

Phone: 770-845-7330

....

13

ENZYMES:
THE KEY TO LIFE AND HEALTH
Joel Robbins, MD, ND, DC

....

In the 1930s very little was known about enzymes,
yet Cayce was once again ahead of his time when, in 1934,
he prescribed an enzyme supplement in one of his readings.

Simone Gabbay, Nutritionist
From: *NOURISHING THE BODY TEMPLE*

Joel R. Robbins, MD, ND, DC, lecturer and writer, focuses his practice on nutrition and wellness. He educates his patients on the art of taking control of their health and the quality of their lives. Robbins earned his Doctor of Medicine from British West Indies College of Medicine, his Doctor of Naturopathy from Anglo-American Institute of Drugless Therapy, and his Doctor of Chiropractic from Cleveland Chiropractic College, Kansas City, Missouri. He is the Director of the Health & Wellness Clinic, Inc., in Tulsa, Oklahoma, and president and founder of the College of Natural Health.

The (Cayce) readings indicate that (raw or lightly cooked) fruits and vegetables should comprise between 60 and 80 percent of the diet.

Eric Mein, MD
From: *KEYS TO HEALTH*

ENZYMES
Joel Robbins, MD, ND, DC

"Within a year of getting out of medical school and setting up practice, I became frustrated, because I was treating patients by drugging them to their next disease," said Joel Robbins, MD, ND, DC. He knew that just palliating symptoms was not health, but he did not know what the answer to wellness was. Robbins was intrigued when he read the US Surgeon General's report. It stated that 7 out of 10 Americans suffer from some chronic degenerative disease. And it ascertained that 75% of all deaths related to stroke, heart disease and cancer could be avoided and often reversed by what people eat or do not eat, regular exercise, sufficient water intake, rest, recreation, stress reduction and no smoking. He sold his medical practice and educated himself about nutrition. Since his medical school education had offered only 6 hours of nutrition classes, "...I had a lot of reading to catch up on, " he explained.

In the course of his extensive studies, he discovered that blood tests of healthy people, unlike blood tests of people suffering from cancer, heart disease, and other illness, contained all the elements found in whole plant food: a full range of vitamins, trace minerals, beta carotene, phytochemicals (plant chemicals), enzymes, other proteins, chlorophyll, antioxidants and soluble fiber. And he learned about the epidemic of hypertension among second generation Africans who did not have hypertension until they came to the USA and ate a typical American junk food diet.

Robbins examined scientific reports about the small fraction of breast cancer in Japanese women who ate a standard Japanese diet. He compared it to the high rate of breast cancer in American women on a standard American diet. The Japanese diet, unlike the American one, was high in complex carbohydrates, rich in fiber and low in unsaturated fats. And he read about many case histories comparing genetically similar people prone to certain disease. The case studies clearly showed that when control in food intake was exercised, the disease could

149

be prevented. "I came to the conclusion that blaming disease on genes was generally an excuse. And I realized that the question we should be asking is, "Did our genes go bad first, or did we treat our bodies so poorly that malnutrition caused our genes to go bad?"

There were many questions that puzzled Robbins. Why, for example, did calves die within six months after being fed a daily diet of their mother's milk heated up to destroy harmful germs? Why would a woman with osteoporosis, trying to help herself by taking calcium tablets, eating ice cream and drinking milk, deplete her bones of more calcium, leading to a worse case of osteoporosis and development of arthritic spurs in her joints? And why did Eskimos, eating a traditional diet of raw whale meat and blubber, a saturated animal fat loaded with cholesterol, have no incidence of cholesterol related disease or heart conditions? Robbins discovered the answer in experiments conducted back in the 40s by Dr. Pottinger. Pottinger, a medical doctor, tried to find out how cooked and processed food affects the body.

Pottinger divided cats into five groups. He fed two groups raw food only, and they remained healthy throughout the experiment. But the other three groups were fed cooked food, resulting in first generation cats developing cancer, diabetes, allergies and other diseases near the end of their life. Second generation cooked-food-fed-cats developed the same chronic diseases in the middle of their lives. And third generation cats had the same diseases when they were born, or within a matter of days or weeks. Many were deformed, had reflex problems and would not play or fight. Third generation cats could not conceive, or they aborted if they became pregnant.

"A common denominator for sustaining good health is live enzymes contained in raw food. Live enzymes help the body break down, dispose of, or put to good use fatty acids from fat, amino acids from protein and sugars from carbohydrates," said Robbins. He suggested trying a simple experiment to prove that cooked enzymes die: boil a seed, then plant it and you will find that the seed will not be able to grow because its enzymes have been deactivated by heat. Similarly, food cooked at 112 degrees Fahrenheit kills its enzymes. Only raw, or lightly cooked food, contains live enzymes which we need for metabolic processes to keep the body alive and healthy.

Not more than a decade ago medical students were taught that enzymes - proteins existing in all living cells, had no medicinal role. It was believed that once they got into the body, they were degraded by stomach acid into amino acid. However, scientists in Japan and Germany proved that theory wrong. "We now know that most of the trillions of catalytic biochemical functions happening every second in the body are reactions predicted by many thousands of enzymes," said Robbins. "Enzymes are the key to life."

150

Robbins decided to pursue formal studies in Naturopathy, completing a residency in Clinical Nutrition, and earning a degree as a Doctor of Naturopathy from the Anglo-American Institute of Drugless Therapy. The practice he subsequently opened focuses on nutrition and education of patients on how to stay well. Robbins teaches patients about the complex subject of enzymes, which he categorizes into two types: metabolic (also known as body enzymes), and plant (also known as food enzymes). Body enzymes are not found in food; only the body can manufacture this type of enzyme. "We are born with a vast supply of stored body enzymes to help bones, tissues, glands and organs carry out metabolic functions to keep us alive," explained Robbins. "To reduce stress on the body, we need an outside source of live enzymes from raw or lightly cooked food. These enzymes convert to metabolic enzymes for replacement of the ones we burn daily."

All essential nutrients, vitamins and minerals are denatured by cooking at high temperatures. Most enzymes are killed when food is processed, chemical-laced, exposed to oxygen, irradiated (the process of exposing foods to high doses of gamma radiation to control pests), pasteurized, microwaved, dried and dehydrated and frozen or steamed, if done incorrectly, depending on the food. According to Robbins, when the body is deprived of live enzymes, it borrows from stored body enzymes in bones, organs and glands to convert dead food into live food. Then metabolic processes can take place to sustain life and health. Abusing the body, year after year, by eating food, vitamins and minerals that are denatured, forces the body to keep borrowing large amounts of body enzymes stored in organs, bones and glands. Unless they are replaced, a body enzyme shortage will eventually occur, impair metabolic functions and lead to disease.

"While you may not miss depleted body enzymes for years, eventually your body will start going down hill, until one day you will be diagnosed with osteoporosis, heart disease or other illness," he says. "The ill effects of a diet of dead food, dead vitamins and dead minerals, are currently taking their toll in twenty-five percent of young adults who are sterile, cannot conceive or miscarry. And these statistics are on the rise." Robbins also says that, presently, children are being born with chronic degenerative disease, juvenile arthritis, juvenile diabetes and a marked increase in type 2 diabetes (commonly known as "adult onset" diabetes) in young children. The leading cause of death for children under age 10 is cancer. "If we compare current health statistics concerning what we are consuming today, with health statistics in 1900 and what people consumed then, it becomes obvious that denatured food, vitamins and minerals are largely responsible for destroying our health."

Robbins also believes that most obesity in America and the industrialized world is caused by the consumption of denatured food, vitamins and minerals.

Obesity is a serious problem, increasing the chances of heart attack by 360%, cancer by 80%, type 2 diabetes by 266%, high blood pressure by 260%, degenerative arthritis by 400% and gall stones by 270%. "If you have tried to cut calories, but cannot lose weight, it probably is because you are eating dead calories," he says. Robbins believes that if live enzymes are not attached to calories, the body will obtain live enzymes from the tissues to convert dead calories into live calories. The body will borrow just enough stored enzymes, for survival that day, to convert some of the dead calories into energy. And the remainder of dead calories are converted into fat. "It takes live enzymes to burn fat cells and get rid of calories," states Robbins. "Eat all the raw fruit and vegetables that you want, and you will not have to count calories."

The medical community generally agrees that there are about 90 nutrients every human being needs daily, 16 different vitamins, 12 essential amino acids, 3 essential fatty acids and 60 minerals, many of which come from the soil. Today, however, supplementation is necessary, because chemical farming has seriously robbed the soil of minerals. For examples, getting the nutritional value you got in 1936 from eating one ear of corn would presently require eating 17 ears of corn. Livestock, feeding on mineral depleted plants, develop nutritional inadequacies, just like people do. Insufficient natural mineral ratios limit the production of enzymes in the body, impeding the function of vitamins. "Fortunately, there are many safe low toxin foods. And we have a choice of eating organically grown food that is produced, processed, packaged, transported and stored without the use of synthetic fertilizers, pesticides, fungicides, herbicides, preservatives, additives, hormones or irradiation.

Robbins says that while nothing beats raw or lightly cooked organic whole food, supplementation of chemical-free live vitamins and minerals has become a necessity. This is true not only because of the poor nutritional value of non-organically grown food, but also because at its best, "the average American spends less then fifteen minutes a day preparing fast processed food for the family, with fresh fruit and vegetables served once or twice every two weeks." Robbins points out that very few vitamin companies understand the concept of live food, live vitamins, live minerals and processing under 112 degrees Fahrenheit, which is expensive and takes more time and effort. FDA regulations allow vitamin companies to produce inorganic processed vitamins and label them "all natural", "which only means that the ingredients originally came from the earth," says Robbins. He recommends researching vitamin companies and asking the right questions to make sure vitamins, minerals and other food supplements you plan to take are truly organic and alive. "Find out about what happens from the time the plant is picked, until it gets into the bottle."

According to Robbins, the average American digests between 30 to 70 percent of what they eat. He illustrates his understanding of the digestion process with an example of eating a raw carrot. Once the carrot has been swallowed and reaches the stomach, the stomach sends out a small amount of body enzymes to activate live enzymes in the carrot for its digestion. When the carrot finishes digesting, the plant enzymes are absorbed into the body as generic enzymes and then convert to body enzymes. A portion of the body enzymes then go back to the stomach to replenish the enzymes used for digesting the carrot. But if the carrot was cooked at high temperatures into a limp denatured state, and then consumed, the body would have the enormous task of digesting the carrot. This would be accomplished by depleting large amounts of stored body enzymes from organs, glands or bones to convert the dead carrot into usable live food.

Many patients and participants at lectures and workshops taught by Robbins have learned how to promote good digestion and diminish excess secretion of minerals. His prescription is for whole, live, organic food and food supplements, sufficient water intake, exercise, no smoking, recreation, adequate sleep, positive thinking, stress reduction and meditation. "My patients reduce high blood pressure, shed extra pounds, elevate their energy levels, rarely get sick and report a general sense of well being," says Robbins.

•••••••••••••••••

Plenty of raw vegetables are to be taken. At least one meal each day should consist wholly of raw vegetables or almost entirely.

EDGAR CAYCE
Reading 1993-1

RECOMMENDED READING

NOURISHING THE BODY TEMPLE:
Edgar Cayce's Approach to Nutrition
Simone Gabbay, R.N.C.P.
A.R.E. Press, 1999

EDGAR CAYCE'S DIET AND RECIPE GUIDE
Compiled by the Editors of the A.R.E. Press
A.R.E. Press, 1999

No Illness which can be treated by diet
should be treated by any other means.

Moses Maimonides
Great Twelfth Century Physician

154

14

PSYCHIC
Letter To Bette Margolis
From Clairvoyant, Rev. Cay Randall-May, Ph.D.

....

Quote from a talk by Edgar Cayce, 1920, from a
Birmingham newspaper article, by Pettersen Marzoni:

"Spiritualism? No. I believe in spirituality... This Cayce you are looking at is nothing. He is but a tool...it is what is done through me as an instrument that counts...I don't count and what you think of what is accomplished through me doesn't count...I don't know what it is that I do, or how it is done. Perhaps Tesla hit it when he said it was like a switch that puts one in contact with the wireless of the universe, or as Edison said there was a record of the universe, and there were needles which fitted the record...I am not trying to get any publicity...if I wanted publicity I could take you out in the street and raise myself 40 feet in the air...I know I can do it. I am not trying to make a fortune out of this power of mine. I refused a theatrical contract a little while ago. It isn't because I am rich. I am poor; I have notes in the bank down in Selma right now. But I am using my power to help whom I can...and I intend to go on doing whatever I can to make the world a little brighter for anyone who is in earnest...I will give no readings that will in the least bring trouble or unhappiness to anyone. I want to help..."

....

Rev. Cay Randall-May, Ph.D, is a clairvoyant, healer and ordained minister. Randall-May began an interdenominational prayer group in 1985. It is the focus of her current independent ministry in the International Council of Community Churches, Phoenix, Arizona. She is the author of *Pray Together Now, How To Find Or Form A Prayer Group* (Element Press). The book documents her experiences in leading a non-denominational prayer group for the past 19 years. In the book, she explores the histories, services and goals of over 90 other prayer groups from various Christian denominations and other faiths. The text also includes an extensive list of Internet prayer group web sites and other prayer resources.

In 1969, she began studying the Bible, praying and meditating as part of an Edgar Cayce Search For God Study Group. After many years of study, she became an ordained minister in 1982. Presently, she holds her ordination with the International Council of Community Churches and the Science of Mind Church for Spiritual Healing. Randall-May is a certified spiritual healer with the Universal Holistic Healers Association and the Independent Spiritualist Association of the USA.

In answer to the question about how
the psychic work is accomplished through
Edgar Cayce's body, Cayce, in trance, said:

...in this [trance] state the conscious mind is under
subjugation of the subconscious minds...or minds
that have passed into the Beyond...What is known
to one subconscious mind or soul is known to
another, whether conscious of the fact or not.

EDGAR CAYCE
Reading 254-2 (2)

Psychic is of the soul; the abilities to reason
by the faculties or by the mind of the soul.

EDGAR CAYCE
Reading 513-1

LETTER TO BETTE MARGOLIS
From Clairvoyant,
Rev. Cay Randall-May, Ph.D.

2001 Mar 03

Dear Bette,

You asked me about my scientific and technical vocation, and how I use my psychic abilities in this regard and in general. My recent scientific research paper published in the *Journal of Scientific Exploration,* illustrates examples of my scientific and technical intuitive work regarding a photochemical solar energy lubricating oil. Both of these were derived through my intuition, and far exceed my conscious understanding or training. Since most of my scientific work is highly confidential, Bette, I am not at liberty to discuss it at this time.

In order to describe what I do as a psychic, I thought I would relate something that happened to me this morning. I received an email from a physician for whom I did a brief reading at a conference last year. I could "see" two fractured ribs on his left side. When I told him about this, he insisted that he was fine and could not remember ever sustaining an injury to his ribs. The email I just received from him, said that his ribs were fractured one month after the reading. This is not the first time that I have "seen" something before it happened. Years ago I did a reading for a woman, and I told her that in the near future she and her husband would be traveling to Japan for a vacation. She "pooh-poohed" the idea, explaining that they could never afford a trip like that. Months later she called to apologize, saying that her husband had won a trip to Japan through his company, and they had really enjoyed touring Japan.

In another instance a woman consulted with me about a future trip that she and her husband were planning. I told her that I saw her making the trip, but without her husband. She asked me to look again, because she thought I had made some mistake, since she never traveled without her husband. I tried, but each time I saw the same thing. Later that year the woman called to say that not long after her reading with me, her husband was suddenly and unexpectedly stricken with a fatal heart attack. She eventually went on the trip without him because she was a widow. These are examples of precognition, which is an inner knowing about what will happen before it occurs.

Sometimes I receive information in unique ways. For example, in October, 1989, I was in the middle of a scientific, technical reading session, when an entity who identified himself as "Chief Seattle" informed me that soon there would be a very strong earthquake in the San Francisco Bay area. This was approximately two weeks before the 1989 Loma Pietra earthquake in California. Chief Seattle told me where and approximately when the quake would happen. The session with him is on tape. And in another scientific, technical session that I participated in, I was similarly interrupted by an image of the Virgin Mary. She said that a war would break out in the Middle East very soon. I received her words one day before Saddam Hussein bombed Kuwait. The Virgin Mary requested prayers for peace from anyone who would listen to her forewarning. I am not Catholic, but I was so impressed by this intuitive session that I immediately began praying for peace. I was stunned when I learned the next day that Saddam's bombs had been dropped.

Psychic abilities are inherited, to some extent, just as athletic or musical abilities often are. Most people are not encouraged to use their psychic talents in their formative years, and some even learn to ignore them. Lack of usage and fear of development would stifle any innate ability. You asked if my family supported my psychic abilities, Bette. Actually, I credit my maternal grandmother, a sensitive herself, for encouraging me to respect my natural intuitive abilities. As a child, we often played games in which we drew on each other's impressions to guess about future events. By the time I reached high school, I had spent several years in the development of my psychic abilities. I aspired to be a parapsychologist when I grew up, but there was little opportunity where I lived for that type of formal study. Instead, I chose to major in biology at college.

In retrospect, I realize that was the right choice. My background in comparative anatomy/physiology, combined with later artistic training, developed a precision in my thinking that complements my clairvoyant abilities when I assess the well-being of my clients during a reading and healing session.

Not everyone recognizes or values my psychic skills. For this reason, I have always felt that people who need my help will seek me out. And those who, for whatever reason, don't appreciate or approve of my abilities will leave me alone. I do not see my work as "fortune telling", and constantly caution people not to give the power of choice to me, the reader. Clients must use the information I give them to make decisions about their options, and then prayerfully decide on what portions of the reading to accept or reject.

I have been doing psychic readings since I was a child. My formal training in mediumship was through the Spiritualist Church. At present I use remote viewing (a modern term for clairvoyance, perceiving objects and events from a distance without the usual senses) as one of my psychic tools. Telepathy, precognition and general intuition also play a large part in my work. I use these methods to assess the flow of chi in a client's energy field. Evaluating a client's auras and chakras also helps me to determine where there is blockage, leakage and weakness in the energy field. The level of activity in the clients' chakras correlates with the level of "openness" to their pertinent issues that need resolution. During a healing session, I intuit the clients emotional and spiritual issues according to my auric perception. With the help of prayer, I clear the field and restore its balance. If the client is receptive, I will use my higher sense of perception to determine what the deeper issues are behind their physical, emotional or spiritual challenges.

Although I do not diagnose illness or recommend medical treatment, I do medical readings on a routine basis. When called upon to give information concerning the physical body, I will, at times, relate extremely detailed descriptions down to the cellular level, or further. Often this information is passed on to a physician who then uses it in evaluating the medical condition.

People frequently consult with me on spiritual matters and ask for assistance in understanding dreams, impressions and higher guidance. Occasionally, past life information enters into my readings and sheds light on how I can help a client comprehend their highest talents, purpose and mission in life and how to receive higher guidance. Some events in our lives are agreed upon, before we enter this plane, between the person's higher self, other entities and guides and teachers in other realms who are assisting with that person's soul growth. Probably this soul-level contract cannot be changed, although other aspects of a person's life are alterable according to free will.

My work is often done in a lightly altered state of consciousness. But sometimes I go so deep that I can reach levels to obtain information useful to medical, scientific and other technical development. It is my belief that when I go this deep, I am in contact with what is known as the "collective unconscious". That is where precise information is available to me that I would not ordinarily be aware of.

Often, I do readings from a distance, usually over the telephone. Occasionally, I give readings through the computer or by creating a tape in response to written questions in which I go with my intuition and include information that "feels" right. I have also participated with a group of psychics who assist in finding missing persons. But I prefer to work anonymously with the authorities in this regard, and seek no publicity. Sometimes I receive information from those who have passed over into other dimensions. However, my training has taught me to be cautious about what I hear. I carefully test the validity of such impressions by requesting detailed and pertinent information, working always with prayer and highest intent.

Over the years I have continued my intuitive evolvement with extensive studies in the area of parapsychology and psychic development. Dream work has also been extremely important to me. In 1973, I began to see auras as a result of a series of dreams which occurred spontaneously. Following Edgar Cayce's advice, I have always sought only the highest good in my intuitive unfoldment. I have asked my guides that I be shown how to serve others with the abilities I possess. Prayer and my continued interest and involvement in art, especially precise drawings, have also contributed to my clairvoyant abilities to depict what I intuitively visualize.

Bette, you asked if I have ever had psychic readings on myself. Rarely, but when I do, it's only because I feel that my intuition is clouded by high emotions. My highest guidance comes in response to prayer and meditation. But I feel that everyone can benefit from brainstorming with others who are qualified and working with integrity. There have been times in my life when I haven't paid attention to my own dream guidance. Years ago, when I was pregnant with my first child, I dreamed of eating refried Mexican beans containing worms. The dream stuck in my mind, because I enjoyed eating refried beans all my life. Sure enough I ignored the warning and ate refried beans at a Mexican restaurant, which caused me to have a terrible attack of gas pain and stomach upset. The problem of bean intolerance lasted throughout that pregnancy, but ever since I have been able to eat Mexican refried beans without a problem.

I have had many impressions that guided me about everyday details, such as which street was safe to drive on. Usually I follow intuitive signs and find that I am in the right place at the right time. Such was the case with my intuition in regard to the Association of Research and Enlightenment, the A.R.E. I first joined the A.R.E., one winter evening in Cleveland, Ohio, in 1969. That night, I had the strong desire to go somewhere, but I didn't know the destination. My husband and I began to ride across town in a snow storm until I saw a small sign in a shop window that said "Food For Body, Mind and Spirit". I knew this was

160

where I wanted to be.

We parked the car, went in, and attended the A.R.E. meeting to organize an Edgar Cayce Study Group. My husband and I joined and participated regularly, once a week, for the next 9 years. It was the Cayce Study Group that lead me to many classes, workshops and development sessions in dream study, Bible study, Cayce remedies and philosophy, the story of Cayce's life and work and other classes related to his readings. Cayce said that psychic development was '...*of the soul*', and that in order for people to improve their intuitive and creative abilities, they must first '...*seek the Kingdom of God within.*' That has always seemed very sound advice to me. It puts emphasis on the wisdom and values needed to use higher sense perception in a healthy balanced way. The A.R.E. has done so much to promote cooperation and information exchange between psychics. And I have assisted in organizing and presenting several professional conferences for psychics at the Virginia Beach headquarters of the A.R.E.

As I see it, my role in life is: fellow-traveler, teacher, healer and spiritual guide It is my hope that others learn to use their high sense psychic perception. It is a natural part of every human being and can be successfully integrated into everyday life. My spiritual beliefs transmit an essential depth to my work and keep me grounded in faith. Psychic abilities are only a tool, in the same respect that eyesight is. It is one's values and ideals that guide us in the way we use these tools to help others in the world. The Cayce readings tell us that the most important thing we can do is to establish an ideal to live by. The ideal may change as one's soul develops. Cayce said, *"Know that the purpose for which each soul enters a material experience is that it may be as a light unto others..."* (641-6).

Blessings,

Cay

•••••••••••••••••

161

Contact Rev. Cay Randall-May at:

PO BOX 31148
Phoenix, AZ 85046-1148
USA
Email: caypraynow@aol.com
fax (602) 404-2191
web site: www.praynow.net

....

RECOMMENDED READING

PRACTICAL INTUITION:
How To Harness The Power of Your
Instinct and Make It Work for You
Laura Day
Villard Books, 1996

THE CONSCIOUS UNIVERSE:
The Scientific Truth of Psychic Phenomena
Dean I. Radin
Harper Edge, 1997

THE INTUITIVE HEART:
How to Trust Your Intuition
for Guidance and Healing
Brenda English and Henry Reed
A.R.E. Press, 2000

THE MIND RACE:
Understanding and Using Psychic Abilities
Russell Targ and Keith Harary
Villard Books, 1984

Index

Nail biting, 7
Nervous system, 126, 127, disturbances, 92
Neural therapy, 79
Neurofeedback, alpha - theta, 70, 71
Neurological problems, 125
Neurotherapy, 67,69,70,71,72,73
New England Journal of Medicine, 7
Numerology, 18 - 34
Nutrition, See diet
Obesity, 151, 152, 152, 153
Osteopathy, 120 - 136
Ovarian problems, 7
Pain, colorpuncture treatment for pain, 93
        diminished pain, 7, 56,
        medicines, 7, 40
        physical, mental, and emotional, 40,
        spiritual pain, 41
Painful intercourse, 7
Panic Disorder, 71
Paralysis, viii.
Parkinson's, viii.
Pavlov, Ivan, 12
Philo, 33
Physical therapy, 125
Plato, 29
PMS, 7, 92
Popp, Fritz Albert, Ph.D., 87, 91
Pouissaint, Alvin F., 16
Prayer, 160
Pregnancy, (in regard to dental care) 138, 139, 140
Priyadarshini Laughter Club International, 13
Protein, 140
Psychic, 155 - 161
Psychoses, 63
Psychotherapy, 94, 95
Puberty, 92
Radiac appliance, vi., vii, viii. ix
Randall-May, Cay, Rev., Clairvoyant, 155-162
Recreation, 153
Reflex points, 80
Reflexology, 63, 79, 89
Relaxation Response, 51, 53, 54, 5

Publisher's Related Books

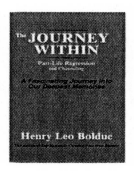

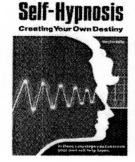

To direct order or contact the publisher
www.TranspersonalPublishing.com

Printed in the United States
53486LVS00014B/79-84